God's Beauty
in the Deep

Raja Ampat, Indonesia

Gary Knapp

COLOR EDITION

WestBow Press books may be ordered through booksellers or by contacting:

WestBow Press
A Division of Thomas Nelson & Zondervan
1663 Liberty Drive
Bloomington, IN 47403
www.westbowpress.com
844-714-3454

Scripture taken from the King James Version of the Bible.

ISBN: 978-1-6642-2310-3 (sc)
ISBN: 978-1-6642-2916-7 (hc)
ISBN: 978-1-6642-2311-0 (e)

Library of Congress Control Number: 2021902690

Printed in China.

WestBow Press rev. date: 04/08/2021

WESTBOW
P R E S S®
A DIVISION OF THOMAS NELSON
& ZONDERVAN

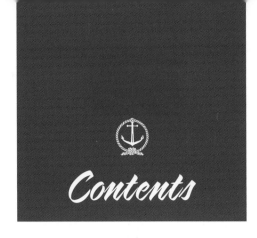

Contents

★ Informational

O Personal Experiences

For in six days the Lord made heaven and earth, the sea, and all that in them is, and rested the seventh day, wherefore the Lord blessed the sabbath day and hallowed it.

—Exodus 20:11

And God said, Let the waters bring forth abundantly the moving creature that hath life, and fowl that may fly above the earth in the open firmament of heaven. And God created great whales, and every living creature that moveth, which the waters brought forth abundantly, after their kind, and every winged fowl after his kind: and God saw that it was good. And God blessed them, saying, Be fruitful, and multiply, and fill the waters in the seas, and let the fowl multiply in the earth. And the evening and the morning were the fifth day.

—Genesis 1:20–23

They that go down to the sea in ships, that do business in great waters;
these see the works of the Lord, and his wonders in the deep.

—Psalm 107:23–24

Acknowledgments

I want to take this opportunity to thank my wonderful family and especially my wife of fifty years of marriage, who allowed me the many opportunities to scuba dive and travel around the world, filming God's wonders in the oceans and seas. I know I missed many events at times due to being away on filming trips. But I felt God's calling to show the world His wonderful creations in another entire world located deep beneath the sea.

Thank you to Morris Langworthy Jr. and Divers Central Inc. in Cadillac, Michigan (www.diverscentral.com) for my dive training. Thanks also to the many dive shops from locations around the world as well as the many dive boats that hosted me in my travels to create the *Dive Travel* series.

Thanks also to Reto Lingenhag, CEO at Education 2000 Inc. in Fort Lauderdale, Florida, for continuing to distribute the *Dive Travel* DVD series around the globe. The DVDs are available individually in both regular DVD and Blu-ray disc as well as in packages by regions of the world at this website: DVDwholesale.net. His email address is reto@education2000i.com.

I would also like to thank you, who are reading this book, and those of you I have met in person, who have demonstrated a keen interest in and support for my many dive films. Also, my thanks go to those of you who have attended my film presentation seminars at various locations in learning about our vast oceans and what God created, as described in the book of Genesis.

I owe a debt of gratitude and a special thank-you as well to Rosemary Logsdon Smith from Sanford, Michigan, who took great time in reading, reviewing, and editing my manuscript.

Thanks also to Hanna Nate and the entire staff at WestBow Press, a division of Thomas Nelson and Zondervan, for publishing this book.

Gary Knapp
Author

A Few Incredible Facts about Our Oceans and Marine Life

 Most of life on earth is aquatic. In fact, 94 percent of the earth's living species exist within the oceans.

 According to the World Register of Marine Species, there are now 240,470 accepted species in our oceans, yet this is believed to be only a fraction of what really exists. Some scientists suggest that there could be millions of marine life-forms out there. New marine life is being discovered every day, with over four hundred different types of sharks alone.

 Sharks are the great police force of the oceans due to their extreme protecting ability. If not for sharks in our oceans, many reefs would die, and many fisheries would go out of business.

 The great white shark, our largest shark today, is an ancestor of the megalodon shark from the prehistoric era. By today's standards, it would make our great white look like a toy poodle. That shark was sixty feet long with 276 three- to seven-inch teeth at any given time. It could swallow a hippopotamus whole and had a bite more powerful than the tyrannosaurus rex.

 The world's longest mountain chain is underwater. The mid-ocean ridge is almost entirely beneath the ocean, stretching across sixty-five thousand kilometers.

 The highest mountain on our planet is Mount Everest at twenty-nine thousand feet high, but if it was located at the bottom of the Mariana Trench in the Pacific Ocean, it would still be covered by over 7000 feet of water. The Mariana Trench, the deepest spot in the ocean, is 11,034 meters or about 36,201 feet deep, which is almost seven miles.

 Not only does a large part of the planet exist beneath the ocean; around fifty percent of the United States does as well.

 Seventy-one percent of the earth is covered by oceans and fresh water, leaving twenty-nine percent as land mass. Humans occupy only ten percent of the earth's surface.

 More than eighty percent of the earth's surface above and below sea level is made up of volcanic origin. There are about fifteen hundred potential active volcanoes worldwide on land, but thousands exist under the ocean, many rising over a half mile above the ocean floor.

 It's possible to find rivers and lakes beneath the ocean. When salt water and hydrogen sulfide combine, the combination becomes denser than the rest of the water around it, enabling it to form a lake or river that flows beneath the sea. There are even waterfalls in the ocean. Technically the earth's largest-known waterfall lies underwater between Greenland and Iceland.

 We need healthy oceans. The ocean is the largest ecosystem on earth; in fact, it is the planet's life support system. Over seventy percent of our planet's oxygen is produced by the ocean. Scientists think that between seventy and eighty percent of the oxygen we breathe is produced by marine plants, nearly all of which are marine algae.

Which ocean is larger, the Atlantic or the Pacific? The Pacific is almost twice the size of the Atlantic, covering about thirty percent of the earth's surface. The second-largest ocean, the Atlantic, with its name referring to Atlas of Greek mythology, covers about twenty-one percent of the earth's surface. While both meet at the southernmost tip of South America, they have no boundaries.

 The third-largest ocean on earth is the Indian Ocean; it covers around fourteen percent of the earth's surface.

 In addition to the oceans, there are seven seas. They include the Arctic, North Atlantic, South Atlantic, North Pacific, South Pacific, Indian, and Southern Oceans. In Greek literature, the seven seas were the Aegean, Adriatic, Mediterranean, Black, Red, and Caspian Seas, with the Persian Gulf thrown in as a sea.

 The Pacific Ocean (meaning "peaceful sea")—the world's largest ocean—contains around twenty-five thousand islands and is surrounded by the Pacific Ring of fire, with numerous active volcanoes.

 Ocean tides are caused by the earth rotating, while the moon and sun's gravitational pulls act on ocean water.

 Less than five percent of the planet's oceans have been explored. The oceans have been less explored than the surface of Venus or Mars. For example, twelve people have set foot on the moon, but only three have been to the Mariana Trench at seven miles deep.

 There are more historic artifacts under the sea than in all the world's museums. Thousands of shipwrecks lie on the oceans' floors.

 The Dead Sea is the saltiest of all seas on the planet, with a thirty-three percent salt level, meaning that most marine life cannot survive there.

 The Bermuda Triangle in the Atlantic and the Dragon's Triangle located in the Devil's Sea close to Japan in the Pacific are located horizontally on the opposite side of the planet from each other. People have reported over the years that planes and ships have mysteriously disappeared in both triangles.

 Ninety-seven percent of all water on earth is ocean water, while only three percent is made up of frozen water and freshwater from rivers and lakes.

 Blue whales have mouths capable of holding you and four hundred of your friends inside, yet they primarily eat one of the smallest animals in the ocean: shrimplike creatures called "krill." They cannot swallow large prey because their throats are only eight inches in diameter.

 The only whale that could swallow a person like Jonah, as depicted in the Bible, would be a sperm whale. This ocean creature has an esophagus capable of swallowing large mammals, but it primarily feeds on large squid and octopus found in the deep.

 Scientists have recently discovered secret rain forests deep within our oceans. According to the World Economic Forum, more than one hundred sixteen coral reefs (unlike coastal coral reefs) have been discovered by submarines diving deep in high seas, between two hundred and twelve hundred meters, where no single nation has jurisdiction.

God's Beauty in the Deep

Chapter 1

A Chilly, Early Morning

I woke up bright and early on a cold morning in June 2009. I was on a one-hundred-twenty-foot liveaboard dive boat as we were closing in on our forty-ninth state, Alaska; we were diving several times a day along the majestic one-thousand-mile Inside Passage. We had started out in Vancouver, British Columbia, Canada, even though summer was just beginning this far north; it was still chilly. Our dive boat eventually passed icebergs and ice floes on the surface of the water passage, which was near the great Le Conte Glacier. For the fun of it, often our captain played music from *Titanic* as we slowly crept past huge, blue-colored icebergs alongside the vessel, setting up a great visual effect as customers on board smiled. Occasionally we saw seals and birds sitting on the floating ice, which later surrounded our boat.

After a quick breakfast, we were busy on the deck, shivering while we slid into our cold dive suits, getting ready to submerge into the dark depths below. On this trip, we were all wearing heavy dry suits we had brought with us, including our specialized dive gear made for cold-water diving. Every time I got into the suit, I wondered why I was diving into cold water again. I had trained in the Great Lakes, where temps were sometimes about the same as here, but it wasn't my favorite type of diving.

Sometimes I wondered why the Lord had sent me to venture into cold regions, but then I remembered that I had long prayed about becoming an underwater videographer. I had promised Him I would show the world His wonders under the vast sea. He reminded me that this was, indeed, part of His many wonders too. I was extremely grateful for all the blessings He had given me in all my diving around the world. What I had seen so far topside, as I gazed at the surrounding snow-capped mountains glistening in the sun, was another beautiful creation He had made. The bright spring flowers and blooming trees bordering the Inside Passage, which meandered through the rugged mountains, offered occasional reflections in the water, which were a sight to behold.

We passed colorful and sometimes well-worn fishing boats, which were out for their day of fishing. They were surrounded by eagles circling in the air around them, all looking for a handout. The ever-changing panorama of natural beauty here came alive as we witnessed hundreds of bald eagles feeding, nesting, and circling overhead. Many trees alongside the passage were covered with eagles, appearing like decorations on a tree. Harbor seals, Alaskan brown bears, humpback whales, and sea otters were seen from time to time—sights that were always entertaining.

But we were all here on a mission this morning, diving to see what awaited us below. It was to be another notorious shipwreck few got to see, since it had sunk so deep in the frigid, icy waters in the late 1800s. While we did all the routine system checks, we all sat in line, awaiting the divemaster's signal to enter the water. It is always a time of excitement and anticipation not knowing what lies below the surface of the waves, which were now rocking our boat.

Finally, one by one we entered the water. Oh, how cold and clammy the water felt! It was around thirty-six to thirty-eight degrees. It felt like a slap in the face, rudely waking us up if we weren't already awake. Even though we were trapped inside heavy rubber dry suits meant to keep us dry from the water, eventually the cold would be felt from the water around us, sending chills down our backs. I thought many times that if only the suit had a heating system, how much nicer the dive would be. With wet suits being used in cold water, some guys literally poured hot water into their suits to prepare for a dive; the water tends to keep them warm for only a little while. But with a dry suit, obviously, you cannot do that. Even though the dry suit kept the main core of our bodies dry, still our faces and hands were totally exposed to the wet, cold water. Of course, we wore face masks and gloves, but they didn't keep the water from touching our skin.

Suddenly, with my heavy, thirty-eight-pound video camera and housing in my hands, we were descending and slowly sinking into the deep water. All we could hear were the air bubbles from our breathing apparatuses coming from the heavy tanks mounted on our backs as we sank deeper and deeper into the darkness. Looking down, I could barely make out the other divers below and ahead of me through the bubbles coming up from divers. The dark, murky water made them look like blurry shadows. It seemed like it took forever to reach our destination as we continued to sink slowly but safely.

Instantly, this giant shadow approached us from below, like a giant monster rising from the depths of the sea. It looked as cold as I felt, built of steel and wood. It was a ship locked in time, a ship that had sunk on its own voyage due to a catastrophic mishap of some kind. It now lay on the dark, deep bottom in such cold water that it stayed intact, preserved as a museum piece for anyone who wished to visit. The sight brought back memories and stories of the famous *Edmond Fitzgerald* and the song by Gordon Lightfoot, who sang the phrase "The lake never gives up her dead."

All we could see were flickers of light and dark shadows emerging from the large vessel. At the depth we were located, there was no longer any visible light. Only our individual dive lights illuminated the object in front of us. It was difficult to see the entire ship all at once. Divers were looking it all over. Sometimes we saw a fish, crab, or an occasional octopus slip around it, evading our bright, beaming lights, which often created an eerie feeling. It was always amazing to me that creatures could live in icy water of thirty-six degrees or less and still be so active. Sometimes my mind wandered, thinking of how many people might have died on board this ship.

We were now on a time limit as to how long we could stay below the surface due to the depth we were in, at one-hundred thirty feet. The cold water on our hands and faces was taking a toll on our bodies. My fingers were freezing as I carried my heavy dive-camera system. Many times when I reached the surface, people topside had to unfasten my dry suit and remove my gloves, since my fingers were so cold and numb that I couldn't move them. The pending hypothermia often dictated how long a diver could stay submersed. But it was all in a day's dive, a work I had relegated myself to, which had started as a hobby.

It was supposed to be fun. That is what all dive classes teach us: if you aren't having fun, don't do it. But many times in certain conditions, I had to ask myself, "Am I having fun yet?" People who indeed know me in the dive industry know me as a warm-water diver, preferring exotic locations with eighty-five-degree ocean temps, lots of sun, beautiful coral reefs, and stunning, colorful marine life. Ahh, that was what I longed for!

Welcome to my world! I had learned a lot from God through all my travels. I had learned the rest from marine biologists I traveled with around the world for over twelve years. I had a large world map mounted on a framed pegboard in my office. Soon each continent around the world would be covered with dive flags, marking every destination I had visited while diving. Also included were all the individual exotic islands He had taken me to.

I have lost count of how many times God has led me on a treasure voyage around the world. Sometimes I traveled to the opposite side of the planet a couple of times each year. I traveled to Australia, Indonesia, the Philippines, China, Japan, Singapore, and many other amazing places. One day I felt like I was in a dream after not more than an hour after getting off a jet plane on the continent of Africa. Being whisked off to Cairo, I found myself sitting on a camel directly in front of the great pyramids of Egypt. Later, I was filming the treasures of the Red Sea.

God truly showed me His world in a tour of the planet, from the topside to the very bottom of His deep ocean creations. He obviously had a plan for my life, and I was grateful for the experience. I have been diving in practically every ocean and most of the seven seas on the planet—north, south, east, and west. And I have filmed most of the popular existing marine life. I have worked alongside famous and experienced underwater videographers from networks like *National Geographic*, the Discovery Channel, and many other filmmakers as well as those who produce pictures for underwater magazines. There are few experiences I haven't had, yet every day is a new one.

I have always worked with gusto and have had a tenacity never to give up filming the best dive locations in the world. But let me explain how this all happened, how I began this long, incredible journey, in which I ended up filming God's awesome wonders and His beauty in the deep.

Chapter 2

The Beginning

Let me tell you a little about myself. I grew up on a small, rural dairy farm in the late '40s to '60s. It was south of Coldwater, located in southern Michigan, just twelve miles north of the Indiana border. I was one of the lucky ones, being born to a great set of parents. I had both a brother and a sister. My brother was fourteen years older, and my sister was eight years older, so I was more alone in later years as a child growing up.

At six years old, I determined I was going to be a radio announcer. I noticed everyone seemed to like listening to the radio for entertainment. I used to pretend to be an announcer and went around interviewing everyone. Of course, this was before television came along. When we got our first TV, the shows were all in black and white. As a youngster, I used to watch a new, weekly show called *Sea Hunt*, starring Lloyd Bridges. I was fascinated by it. I always thought scuba diving would be a fun and interesting thing to do someday, if I ever got a chance to experience it. Looking back, I can see how that show planted a seed deep within me that would someday launch me into a new hobby. But little did I know just how far it would lead me.

During my preteen years, my mom dragged me to church. I thank God for that now, although at the time I wasn't too happy. As a small, barefoot boy growing up on a dairy farm, *There are far too many things to do,* I thought, *rather than sit in church with no one I really know.* But soon I found a youth group of kids my age, with whom I readily made friends and got involved.

One year they held a fundraiser and gave me small pictures of Jesus in various poses to sell: Jesus knocking at the door, Jesus in the garden, and so forth. They were five-by-seven, designed, cardboard-framed prints; and I went around the neighborhood selling them. Back then, there were no worries of safety; people didn't even lock their doors. It was a time of innocence and peace in our country when neighbors and relatives dropped by without having to request an invitation.

I apparently did well with my early salesmanship; I won a prize in my youth group. It was a thirty-three LP of music from the religious recording artist George Beverly Shea. I took it home and played it and fell in love with the low dulcet tones of his soothing voice. It was the only record I owned, and I played it on our old record player repeatedly, singing along with it. As a tutor, unbeknownst to him, Mr. Shea was my inspiration and introduced me to music early on. He gave me the idea of wanting to become a singer. It was his voice alone, along with those special words in the music, that years later brought me to knowing Christ as my personal Savior around the age of nine.

As a teenager, I began singing solos in church. My first solo was George Beverly Shea's "The Wonder of It All." He not only recorded this song, but it was also the only one he personally wrote. I was invited to sing other songs of his and finally was asked to lead the singing for the general congregation at Lockwood Community Church, where I also started singing duets with a girl from our youth group.

In the '60s, the Vietnam War was brewing, and the United States had a draft that was in full effect. I had registered, and my number was coming up. I decided to enlist, rather than wait to be drafted, because I was told, "If you enlist, you have a better choice of a vocation within the army." I guess it worked; the army said I was best suited to be in the clerical field as a typist. *Really?* I thought. *A boy from the farm who had never taken a typing class in high school?*

I went to basic and AIT training (Advanced Individual Training) at Fort Knox, Kentucky, where I was in a barracks with all southern boys from southern parts of the USA. In just six short weeks of basic training and another six weeks of advanced, technical training, I managed to quickly pick up their southern accent. I remember thinking, *How will I ever make it as a radio announcer in northern states sounding like this?* It took me several years to rid myself of that southern drawl.

Instead of sending me to Vietnam, the army sent me to Germany for the entire three years of my enlistment at the seven hundred and ninth Military Police Battalion. I remember feeling guilty at the time I received my orders. Being raised on a farm where we worked together as a team, I was raised such that we all supported one another. How was it that I was being sent to Germany while my newfound southern buddies, with whom I had spent six weeks in training, were all going to Vietnam? I was so ashamed and disappointed. I never told anyone I was going in the opposite direction; I had always assumed we were all going to war, even though my home church had prayed I wouldn't. God had indeed apparently spared me.

Meanwhile, in Germany I moved around to many different locations but ended up in WIldflecken, in the mountains, for the first year. I got a taste for traveling when a German friend of mine, who worked with me as an interpreter for the military police, took me to the surrounding countries on some weekend vacations during my three-year enlistment. We traveled in his small Volkswagen Beetle to the surrounding countries of Austria, Belgium, Denmark, Norway, Sweden, Amsterdam, Holland, France, and even Iceland for two days on the way during a trip back home. I invited him to go home with me during my month-long vacation from the army, since he had never visited the USA.

I joined a military chapel at my base in Wildflecken and was soon singing lead in a quartet. We were like an extended family over there within the small church. We got to know the families of many of the military men and women. My chaplain, Captain Barnes, a Southern Baptist minister, whom I really enjoyed, later baptized me by immersion on October 9, 1966, along with others in a cold, German river nearby. I felt totally committed to Jesus and to the Christian life.

It was about that time that we had a special visitor as a guest preacher at our service one Sunday night. Our special speaker had been released just twenty years prior from a German prison camp during the Holocaust. Her family had helped Jews escape the Nazis from the Holocaust during World War II. She and her family had been arrested for housing Jews in their home, which had secret rooms above a clock shop in Holland. The family was believed to have helped as many as eight hundred Jews. She wasn't well known yet, but later she certainly would be. Her name was none other than Corrie ten Boom.

Having already lost both of my grandmothers, I loved her grandmother-style image immediately. We stood in line to greet her after her talk to our small congregation until finally she stood there in front of me—this Dutch-born, Christian lady with the greatest, beaming smile you can imagine. While taking hold of my hands, she asked me what I wanted to do in life. I told her I wanted to be either a religious singer or a radio announcer following my service in the army. I was impressed that she held my hands while we talked and later even hugged me before leaving but not before she told me, "With God's help and blessings, you could do anything with Him and through Him." I was always very inspired by her and her comments, even though at the time of our meeting I didn't know a lot about her. But our meeting later had a great impact on my life, when I thought back on what she had told me, especially coming from a woman who had been through so much pain and suffering and even lost her family while in her prison camp. I have since then seen her movie, *The Hiding Place*, and read all her books.

Corrie lost both her father and her sister to that camp, where she and her sister ministered to many of the women in the camp after smuggling in a small Bible and leading them to Christ. What was most inspiring was that Corrie was released only due to a clerical error mix-up by the Germans at the last minute. It happened just one week before they killed all of her roommates, which were in the barracks of her age-group, in the gas chamber. There were one thousand two hundred of them. But God had a plan; He wanted her to be released to share and to tell her story to the world—and that she did. Later in 1975, her movie, *The Hiding Place*, was released. It was filmed by the production crew of World Wide Pictures, the production company of the Billy Graham crusades, where she also appeared many times. She went on to write many books, including *The Hiding Place, Tramp for the Lord, Prison Letters, In My Father's House, Amazing Love, Not Good If Detached*, and many others. These books tell the story about her life in the prison camp and share the great faith that carried her through those rough years. I was blessed and inspired by her, realizing I had met her long before the rest of the world came to know her.

Corrie ten Boom

Following my four-year stint in the army, I attended a radio and television broadcast academy. I worked in radio for sixteen years, then built a Fox television station after many prayers and with the help of God. It took us seven years for God to answer that prayer. It is the subject of my first book, *Building the American Dream.* I completed another sixteen years in television before selling the station in early 2000. During my broadcast experience, I got married and had two beautiful daughters. Now I have six wonderful grandchildren. I am proud to say that two of my youngest grandchildren, Jessica and Michael, are helping me with the production of this book.

As I mentioned before, I wrote a book called *Building the American Dream* from AuthorHouse Publishing following my broadcast career. It is still available online and at bookstores like Amazon.com, Barnes & Noble, and Authorhouse.com as well as other major bookstores. The book describes the first part of my life while growing up on a farm; it includes school, the service, Germany, plus my sixteen years of radio and my sixteen years of cable TV and broadcast television. The state chamber of commerce told me once that the book is also a good resource, a business manual for anyone starting up a new business, since the same principles exist; mine just happened to be TV stations. With no help from the banking community, I had to form a limited partnership to raise the necessary funds to eventually build the stations, so there was a definite learning curve. It took seven long years, and it happened only through my faith in God.

Now I begin again with this second book, a continuation of *Building the American Dream*, which is part of my lifelong journey with my new hobby, scuba diving. I never discussed scuba diving in my first book, since I hadn't yet started that hobby, but that is what this book is all about and where it all began. In it I share my vast experiences of learning to dive and the thirty-seven hour-long shows I later made, called *Dive Travel*, which I filmed around the world over a twelve-year period.

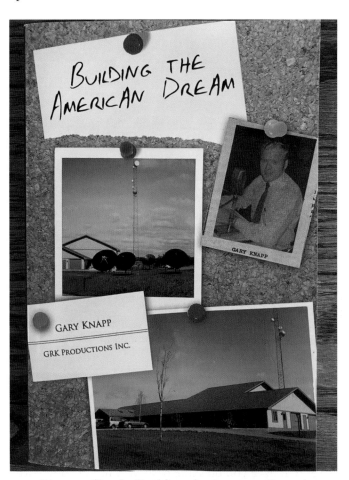

Picture of book (*Building the American Dream*)

Chapter 3

Preparing to Dive

After selling the TV station in the year 2000, I was suddenly and officially retired. I was out of a job for the first time in my life at age fifty-four. My retirement started off abruptly by my having unexpected open-heart surgery. The heart doctor said I had the heart of a nineteen-year-old. Since I had never had a prior heart attack, with his catching this one in time, my heart was renewed following a triple-bypass surgery. In a few months, I was back to my normal exercise and wondering what God had planned for the second part of my life.

For a few years, I talked to high school and college students as a motivational speaker, trying to instill in students the concept of believing in themselves, as I had done. It is amazing how many kids today have such low self-esteem. I told them to always follow their dreams, to set goals in life, and to never give up on them, for once they give up, those dreams will be lost forever. I reminded them that many adults complain about their jobs when they are the ones who chose that path. I always looked forward to going to work each day, and if you cannot say that, then maybe you chose the wrong career.

Later, I had an extensive hobby garden for seven years—almost like a truck garden, from which I offered produce from the farm. But, tiring of that, I began to think about that diving show called *Sea Hunt,* starring Lloyd Bridges. I remembered it from my youth and the interest it had once generated in me.

I had interviewed a dive instructor during my years as a talk-show host on radio and television. Morris had been in the navy during his service years and had gone about as far as one can go in the diving industry. He achieved the top title of a PADI course director, a class far above most instructors. PADI is the Professional Association of Diving Instructors. Northern Michigan is lucky to have him, since there are few course directors in the entire country, let alone Michigan. His dive shop not only offers training for new divers but also trains instructors; it also offers advanced training for all police and emergency service workers, who work search and rescue for drowning victims. I was always impressed with his expertise and had the greatest respect and admiration for him and his dive shop. Soon I would be taking his classes, since he owned the local dive shop in Cadillac, my hometown.

In taking the basic PADI course for an open-water diver, I never realized in just a little over one year I would end up having completed not only the basic open-water course but also twelve additional advanced courses.

First, I took the basic course, half of which was book work; then it was pool experience, followed by entering a freshwater lake nearby. To become a scuba diver, you first need to feel comfortable in the water and have basic swimming skills. Your instructor will have you do some basic swimming and floating exercises but nothing too extreme.

The equipment you will need, which the dive shop usually supplies when you take a course, includes a mask, fins, and snorkel—unless you have your own, which is recommended for sanitary reasons—along with a wet suit and dive boots. Other items you need include a BCD (a buoyancy compensator, also known as a buoyancy control device), a harness system that goes over your shoulders, which holds the air tank that fits on the back of it. Lastly, but most importantly, you need a regulator as part of the streamlined equipment, which allows you to breathe underwater. It attaches between the BCD device and the air tank. You also need a dive computer or at least an air gauge, which tells you how much air you have in your tank along with other vital information.

Just to take a basic course to decide whether you want to become a scuba diver, the dive shop supplies everything. So there are no worries about obtaining it all upfront. Even when you are traveling around the world, it's not necessary to bring your own gear, unless you want to, since most dive shops have all the gear you'll need as rental gear. Most serious divers, however, carry their own equipment; they are more comfortable owning their own. Once you become a diver, you will find many more items to add to your dive equipment needs along the way.

You might seem overwhelmed at first, realizing you need to wear these things to learn to scuba dive. However, it is more lightweight under the water, and eventually the equipment becomes second nature to you, like driving a car. The feeling is very strange the first time though. The mask and awkward gear may feel a bit heavy on you before entering the water. As you ease into the water and your face slips below the surface, you inhale, and the air comes with a reassuring hiss. For the first time, you breathe underwater, and in a mere moment, you forget your mask. The equipment transforms, becoming light and agile, and you are free like you have never experienced before. With that first underwater breath, a door opens to a whole new world.

Once you experience diving, your life will never be the same again. It is a totally new adventure bringing you close to nature. God's beautiful corals and the multitude of colorful sea life will astound you to no end. As you travel to different countries and dive destinations, each will be a special place and challenge. God reigns over all the seas and has created underwater mountains and sheer cliffs with drop-offs to deep trenches and valleys, the same as you see above when traveling—all of which makes you feel totally at peace, be it swimming under the ocean, catching a current, or drift diving. There are so many ways and options available for you to experience what lies beneath the crystal-clear sea and in its depths below.

You have probably seen footage of dives on television or in films, but until you experience it yourself, you have no idea just how magnificent it can be. Every dive location offers something special and unique under the water. Just as on land, you have different tourist attractions across our planet—the Grand Canyon, the cactus and deserts in Arizona, the Rocky Mountains in Colorado, the volcanoes in Indonesia, and various attractions across the globe. So does the ocean offer unique experiences. Every dive offers something special to see. It is through this series that I get the opportunity, as a tour guide, to take all of you along with me to see and tour the world together—from the very top of mountains to the deepest trenches in the ocean, from looking down inside volcanoes and seeing the red-hot lava flow out to the sea to diving inside a volcano under the ocean and feeling the boiling water emerge, from witnessing God's most beautiful soft-coral flower gardens in Fiji to the marine life under the icebergs of Alaska. If you are ready to traverse the planet, then come along with me for this amazing adventure.

Diving is one of those rare activities that delivers either adrenaline and intensity or serenity and peace. Training through PADI or other licensing firms can take you from a beginner to as advanced a diver as you want to become. Technical divers go even deeper than recreational divers, who can dive to a depth as low as one hundred thirty feet. Technical divers go down far below that, so whatever your interest is, like most any sport, you can take it as far as you want in your exploration of the magnificent oceans and seas that surround us or the many freshwater lakes around the world.

Having taken my course during the winter in northern Michigan, my instructor was planning a trip to Cozumel, Mexico. He invited me and some other dive students to go with him to the island to finish the course. This would allow us both the experience of diving in the salt water of the ocean and complete the course in warm weather at the same time. In the summertime, we would normally just go to an inland lake for this last training exercise.

Well, it didn't take me long after seeing God's beauty under the ocean—the beautiful coral reefs and millions of colorful fish of all types and sizes—I was hooked. I knew this was going to end up giving me great joy. I thanked God for the experience, but I didn't realize just how involved I would later get. I can remember our final, deep dive in the ocean there before I completed my first course.

My instructor took me down deep to see whether I was susceptible to nitrogen narcosis; it would be a test. It has an extreme effect on one's body when doing deep dives. It's not for anyone afraid of going down deep under the ocean. Going below the recommended depths of one hundred thirty feet as a recreational diver sometimes causes divers to begin to feel and act like a drunk person—slowly losing one's thinking ability, which can be dangerous if you are alone. It usually kicks in at depths of one hundred thirty feet. As a new diver, that's the deepest I had ever been. We were on a cliff much like a cliff hanging off a mountain, only deep under the ocean. Just like mountains located on the surface of the earth, there are mountains and cliffs below the ocean. I remember hovering over the cliff that day, which my dive instructor said dropped five thousand feet or more below us to the bottom.

I don't remember the outcome, but I think I got through it okay. All I could see was very dark, deep water with an endless, unseen bottom below. I wondered what frightening things must live below what we couldn't see. I knew then that, if I were to sink to the bottom, no one could ever come down to save me, since no one could ever venture that deep to recover a body. There are limitations to just how deep one can descend in a rescue attempt. I was told that sometimes the water is so crystal clear that divers don't realize how deep it is. Divers must watch their dive computers carefully and not get distracted. It would be easy for that to happen.

I have seen it myself many times when I was deeper than I thought I was until I checked my depth. I was told that at the time eleven hundred divers descended each day under the ocean from that island, and that is a lot of divers. But sadly approximately twelve divers disappeared each year by diving there. I was also informed that sometimes people committed suicide by simply going down deeper and deeper until they passed out and eventually sank to the bottom, never to return. Knowing there were bodies lying down there in their final resting place, five thousand feet down or deeper, gave me a creepy yet sad feeling. I have thought many times about the deepest parts of the oceans and what must lie down there below what we can see.

The Mariana Trench lies just south of Japan and east of the Philippines. You can look it up on a world map. I was near that location during future dives in my later years of travel, but this location is the deepest the ocean ever gets. That's thirty-six thousand and seventy feet deep. It's hard for anyone to imagine or comprehend that depth. To better comprehend it, consider that there are five thousand two hundred eighty feet in a mile, so this equates to seven miles deep. To put that in perspective, consider this. The next time you look up at the heavens and see that tiny, high-flying jet sparkling in the sky above, which the sun reflects off of and you can barely make out, remember, it is flying at or about thirty thousand feet above the earth. Even that distance is six thousand feet less than the ocean is deep.

So think of it like this: if you were standing on the ocean's bottom in the Mariana Trench and looked up toward the surface, where the waves were rolling, it would be that deep just to get to the surface. The *Titanic* is located about three hundred fifty miles south of the Island of Newfoundland in about twelve thousand five hundred feet of water; even that far down is only one-third of the depth of the Mariana Trench. Mount Everest, the world's highest mountain, is twenty-nine thousand feet tall. If it were placed at the bottom of the Mariana Trench, it would still be covered by seven thousand feet or almost two miles of water!

Can you even comprehend the total weight of that much water at that depth? Specially designed submarines need to be heavily constructed to withstand the incredible, intense pressure due to the weight of the water above. I guess that is the adventure of diving, always wondering what lies below the surface you cannot see. Today man knows more about Mars and outer space than about what lies beneath our oceans, which for the most part haven't been explored.

Chapter 4

Open Water

I laugh now when I think back on my first diving course: open water. I thought that was a challenge for me, with it being my first time under water. I certainly had no idea what was in store for me in the form of more courses I would end up taking later that same year. Looking back, I think I had become a glutton for punishment.

The twelve courses I took are as follows: Open Water Diver, Advanced Open Water Diver, Enriched Air Diver, Specialty Diver, Dry Suit Diver, Specialty Diver Deep-Sea Diver, Specialty Diver Night Diver, Specialty Diver Underwater Videographer, Specialty Diver Search & Recovery Diver, Enriched Air Nitrox Diver, Primary & Secondary Care CPR First Aid/AED, Rescue Diver, Divemaster, and finally, Master Scuba Diver. Had I taken just one more course, I would have ended up being an instructor myself. That, however, never appealed to me. I had, in fact, taken all the courses I could handle, both physically and mentally, and all were in just one year's time. I think I even surprised my instructor—possibly setting a record for the number of courses taken in such a short time frame, especially at my age.

Most people learning to dive take only the first course. Open water is really all that is required to go recreational diving. With it, you get a certified card that allows you to go to any dive shop, get air in your tank, and be certified to dive almost anywhere in the world. However, the need for more training is required for more serious, deeper dives.

After returning from my first trip out of the country and having taken some of the more advanced courses mentioned above, I read many books on diving with great interest. One in particular talked about the need to take a rescue diving course to know what to do in case a dive buddy suffered a seizure or heart attack while under the ocean and how to try to save or rescue him. I thought about that issue for a long time, and it weighed heavily on me. I tried to visualize how awful I would feel if someone diving with me suffered a heart attack or illness under the water and I didn't know what to do to help him or her and how terribly guilty I would feel if I couldn't save him or her.

I also gave some thought to the interest I had in filming under the ocean as a videographer. Since I had been involved in video and cameras with the TV station over the past sixteen years, I thought about showing others God's wonders under the deep. *Maybe this is what God is training me for, something most non-divers don't get a chance to see*, I thought. I had to admit that after first seeing the beautiful coral and marine life God had created in my very first ocean adventure, I was pretty much hooked on wanting to capture those sights for others to see. My instructor agreed with me and encouraged me by saying, *If I was going to travel around the world scuba diving, I should have the knowledge on how to rescue someone or even myself.* Upcoming dive trips with a variety of situations and different dive buddies could be a risk. I had no idea I would end up having hundreds of dives under my belt before I was done filming. My decision to take the rescue courses paid off. I felt as prepared as I could possibly be in the event that I needed the expertise while diving on locations.

A divemaster is the so-called leader most dive boats on ocean voyages employ; he's the guy who offers you safety instructions on the boats before you snorkel or dive. And sometimes he leads the dives underwater. To become a divemaster, one first needs to take a rescue diver course, CPR course, and other courses that lead up to this level of diving. I found the rescue diver course to be the most physical and intense course I had ever taken or been involved in. Besides being a rescue diving course, it was also a course designed to teach me how to survive should any emergency arise.

The rescue diver program prepares you to help prevent and, if necessary, manage dive emergencies, minor and major, with a variety of techniques. It gives you confidence as a diver and better prepares you in general. For example, part of the course teaches you what to do if someone is drowning and how to carefully swim out to him or her safely. Drowning victims panic and grab at anything and everything and even climb on top of you just to get out of the water, possibly drowning you at the same time or clawing at you or pulling off your mask. The situation can be dangerous, even though you are trying to help the victim. Many people without this training have died while trying to save a drowning victim. So one needs to know how to swim around or under victims, grab them from behind, and rescue them while keeping them afloat and bringing them in to shore. At the same time, the rescuer must remain safe. For a worst-case scenario, the training even offers how to do a search and rescue to retrieve the body of a drowning victim. It's a real learning experience most people have no idea about.

In a further rescue example as part of the course, my dive buddy, who was also taking the course with me, and I were anxiously awaiting a swim out in Grand Traverse Bay one afternoon in Lake Michigan. We were on the shoreline, sitting on the tailgate of my F150 truck with our dive gear in the back. We were still dressed in our clothes, since we weren't allowed to be already in our diving gear during this training exercise. This was a challenge test on how quickly we could suit up and get out in the water for our first rescue dive attempt.

The diver, whom we will refer to as Rick, was in the water a long way from shore; he signaled to us that he was ready to be rescued. He immediately submerged and rested on the bottom with his diving gear on to await our arrival and "rescue." We quickly suited up, putting on our dive suits and BCDs,--the vests that held our tanks and air supply connecting us to the tanks. Taking our masks, snorkels, and fins, we quickly got out in the water as fast as possible. We were being timed to see how long it took us to find him, check his vitals, and get him safely to the surface while floating him back to shore, where we would, if it was a real emergency, call 911.

We immediately swam to the location where we thought we had seen him go down. That was a challenge in itself, since distance plays a trick on you sometimes, especially on a large body of water like this. We tried to use the line-of-site technique we had been trained in and eventually found him lying on the bottom, probably sleeping while waiting for us. He was supposed to be pretending to need a rescue, and I am sure he was smiling or laughing at us.

We checked his vitals and air supply. We signaled that we were there as rescue divers to take him to the surface. We then added air in his BCD and slowly took him up. Now the real work began. Not only was the water rough, with two- to three-foot waves, but we had to hold his head up above water as we floated him to shore so he wouldn't drown after bringing him up safely. We certainly didn't want to drown him after just saving him from certain death. We had to pretend to do mouth-to-mouth resuscitation CPR, counting in between breaths, while at the same time swimming with him and pulling him toward the shore. While doing these continuous steps, we needed to remove all his dive gear from his body and take off his BCD, tank, fins, and so forth. Along with these tasks, we had to get our own heavy gear off at the same time while doing CPR and swimming in high waves. The fins would be removed last as we neared shore, since we still needed them to swim.

The gear had to be removed while in the water from both of us, the victim and the rescuer, since we had to be able to pick him up and carry him to shore. When we reached shore, we had to pretend to call 911, all while continuing to do CPR. With the equipment still on each of us, it would have been impossible to stand up, pick him up out of the water and then place him on dry land. I had to wonder what people on shore must have thought had they witnessed us trying to rescue a diver, not knowing whether it was real. I am really surprised someone didn't call 911.

I have to say that at my age, then close to fifty-eight, it was one of the most challenging and physically draining events I had ever accomplished in my life. I am sure that had I been younger, it would have been a little easier. After that episode, I decided I certainly wouldn't want to be a rescue diver as a full-time career. However, I learned to respect all rescue divers who work in that field. Thankfully, I was doing this exercise only for the course itself, so I could learn what I needed to know if ever I was put to the test for a real rescue attempt. I prayed to God that day would never happen and that I would never have to do that again in my lifetime. Since I was at the early threshold of my diving experience, time certainly would reveal that answer in the future.

On becoming a divemaster, we were expected to do some internship training of sorts by going out with our instructor and his new students to assist them and check them over to make sure they were prepared for their first underwater training. Oh my, how it brought back many memories of our first-time experiences of learning to dive all over again!

Chapter 5

Diving Experiences

Whenever possible, one of the biggest dangers to avoid while swimming at a beach is rip currents. In the United States rip currents kill more than one hundred people each year and account for some eighty percent of the rescues performed by lifeguards. Sometimes lifeguards will mark certain areas along the beach as unsafe rip current areas. The currents can be seen if you really pay attention to the shoreline. They act like a river flowing outward. Signs of one include bits of debris or a line of foam moving seaward. Or it may appear as a channel with fewer breaking waves in what looks like a river of darker water flowing out to sea.

The best way to escape a rip current is to avoid swimming in it altogether. However, if you find yourself caught in one, the best advice is to not panic while being pulled out to sea from the beach. Obviously, one may be frightened at first, but try to stay as calm as possible. You do not have to be a strong swimmer. Instead, just float on top of the water. If you have a floatation device, hold on to it, but if not, no worries just try and float.

The currents will not pull you under. Instead raise your hand over your head to alert others and yell for help. Try to swim parallel and work your way to the right or left of the rip to get out of the menacing current. Never swim back directly against the current—which most people attempt to try—since the water is usually moving out faster than you can swim against it. Some divers say it may be better to just float and do nothing.

Those studying rip currents have discovered eighty to ninety percent of rips flow in huge circles from the shallows out through the breakers and back again every few minutes. The rip may bring you right back toward the beach once out of the current. The biggest mistakes made by people unfamiliar with rip currents are trying to rescue someone in a panicked situation and finding themselves caught up in the same current. I have known people who have died trying to rescue family members in that manner.

When you first learn to dive, you are taught about an important part of diving—it's all about proper buoyancy and what being in the water as a scuba diver means. There are three different types of buoyancy that are of importance. Positive buoyancy refers to a diver floating upward toward the surface. Negative buoyancy is when a diver sinks toward the bottom. And neutral buoyancy is when a diver neither sinks nor floats but instead is neutral or in between. A diver without good buoyancy is like a driver out of control. This is one who is unable to change lanes, go in reverse, or parallel park. Overall, this isn't a very good diver.

I have heard people say, "If you are heavy, you will sink like a ton of bricks in the water." In fact, the situation is just the opposite. You will float like an inner tube or a giant bobber. I hate to say it, but the blubber on your body will make you float like a whale. I can remember one occasion when I had to assist a young guy who was very much overweight, but he was a big, husky, burly football player type. Here is an example of what most people don't understand. The more you weigh, the more weight you need on you to hold you down when diving. In his case, the man needed about fifty or more pounds of added weight on a weight belt around his waist. On the other hand, a normal-sized person of about one hundred sixty pounds might need only an extra ten to fifteen pounds or less.

Think of a person's body like a fishing bobber floating on the surface of the water when you put lead weight on a line under it. When fishing, the weight pulls the bobber down; the more weight you put on, the deeper the bobber goes. Likewise, it is the same with a diver. The average diver may have an extra four to twelve pounds or more of weight on him or her; once divers get more comfortable with added experience in the water, using a relaxed breathing technique, they can sometimes wear less weight as long as they have enough weight to take them down to the bottom after letting all the air out of their BCD floatation devices.

The way to test if you are properly weighted as a diver is to get in the water with all your gear on and let out all the air in your BCD vest. If you sink to eye level or below, you are usually okay, but if you float above that on the surface and cannot get down, you need to add more weight to your weight belt. A standard rule is to always be a little bit over weighted, since there are certain times when you may run into problems with currents and other issues, and extra weight comes in handy.

On this occasion, I felt sorry for the young guy who had to have so much weight attached to him just to take him down. His weight belt kept falling off once he was in the water; he had to carry it when getting ready to descend. And guess who had to go down and retrieve the weight off the ten-foot bottom of the lake? You guessed it, the assisting divemaster. I couldn't even lift the heavy weight off the bottom to come to the surface. All I could do was drag it up toward the shore in shallow water each time, which was now numbering several attempts. He tried many times to get it to stay on and eventually succeeded. But lightweight guys and girls need to have enough weight to be able to descend properly. It is a learning experience for every diver no matter his or her size or age.

It's amazing how much pressure is involved in the weight of the water for every ten feet you descend. We used to take an empty plastic water bottle down to the bottom, and it would collapse under the pressure. Or break an egg underwater and see what happens; the egg stays intact and won't break. Colors change at various depths as well. A red fishing lure found on the bottom looks black until you bring it to the surface. Colors change and eventually disappear at every depth. The longest wavelengths, with the lowest energy, are absorbed first. Red is the first to be absorbed, followed by orange and yellow. The colors disappear underwater in the same order that they occur in the color spectrum. Even water at a five-foot depth will have a noticeable loss of red.

Learning to become an underwater videographer was a real challenge in the beginning. I had operated many camera systems all my life in still photography and video for the television station. Filming on bare ground or from platforms is relatively easy, but I would soon find out filming under the ocean was an entirely different situation. First, you need to be an excellent diver and get experienced in that alone, which takes time. It's like taking baby steps; at first no one is a natural at it. Once you know how to dive and have proper buoyancy under the ocean, you can then, and only then, concentrate on taking pictures. Safety is always a priority. I have seen some photojournalists get so involved in their work that they lose track of safety regulations like neglecting their air supply and finding it running low, not checking their computer, or worse yet, getting lost going out on their own or leaving their dive buddy alone. Those mistakes might be fine if you are a divemaster and have all the training, but an open-water diver with little experience can get into real trouble quickly.

Practicing buoyancy is another course in itself. When you are down on the bottom of the ocean floor, you cannot be kicking into coral reefs, since many reefs are in marine parks, and you aren't allowed to disturb the reef system. But many times new divers don't know how to stay off the bottom without proper training, so they rile up the bottom, making it unpleasant and difficult for other divers nearby to see. There are courses to take in which you learn to swim through hoops underwater and to avoid touching the hoop as you swim through it. It takes practice, but when you are on the bottom and are approaching a reef or various corals you want to swim over, simply inhale and put air in your lungs, and you will slowly rise above the reef and clear the vegetation. To go back down, exhale, and you will slowly descend as fish do.

You can also use your BCD device to add or decrease air from your vest to achieve the same result. Once you become comfortable with it, just your breathing alone will do the job. It takes a while to feel comfortable. At certain depths, many breathe in too much air from rapid, deep breathing; this will drain your air tanks, cutting into your bottom time and requiring you to surface before the rest of the dive group, ending your dive. You need to learn to breathe slowly in a relaxed style to save air supply. Of course, that is easier said than done when you're fearful of the unknown below you, especially when confronting a shark.

I had to laugh when I tried my first attempt at taking still pictures under the ocean. I thought that, since I was a television person with camera and video experience, I would be a natural at this. Ha ha! I was so naïve! I had no clue what I was getting into.

Something happened during my first trip to the ocean in Cozumel, Mexico, when I went down with my dive instructor to finish my first open-water course there. I had bought one of those cheap disposable cameras they sell tourists who are on vacation on exotic islands. I took it down on a dive one day and took pictures; I thought they would be good shots of colorful fishes and reefs I encountered, thinking, *Wow, this is so easy!* After all, it looked easy when I was taking them through the cheap lens. But upon surfacing and later having the photos developed, I found that few of the pictures were even viewable—certainly nothing I wanted to show anyone. I found that getting pictures under the ocean would require practice, since you need to be a whole lot more focused on the efforts and make sure you are much closer to the subjects to get good quality. You also need good filters to retain color in the deep as well as a good lighting system. Finally, you need a good-quality underwater camera housing, which requires training to use in itself before going down below, since the housing gives added weight to your dive. But mostly you just need to be a really good diver. Experience sometimes takes years.

It took me several years before I felt really comfortable and began to get good-quality video. I wasn't into still photography underwater; I preferred video—showing realistic action shots and movement of the marine life, reefs, and other divers under the ocean in an attempt to show what it really looks like to dive. I started out with a cheaper video system in digital video, but later, once I got more experience, I invested in a much larger and higher-tech Sony video camera and bought a professional Gates underwater housing for it with a super, wide-angle lens. At the time, HD (high definition) widescreen had just come into play, and now the video became crystal clear. Then I found a new exercise to get used to as my complete system with lights, camera, and housing now weighed about thirty-eight pounds, much heavier than my starting system, and much larger to push under the ocean. But soon I got used to it, and underwater, it was negative buoyant, meaning it virtually floated underwater. I was using more air, however, to push it through the water, since it wasn't very aerodynamic.

Blu-ray was just being developed as a new distribution service on DVD, introduced by Sony, and we wanted to be one of the first companies to produce our underwater films in HD widescreen and to be released on Blu-ray disc. Today all but the first six of our thirty-seven shows are available on Blu-ray. I always thought there were a lot of professional videographers out there, making underwater films. But once I gained experience, I found myself at the time diving alongside famous photographers from the Discovery Channel, the National Geographic Channel, individual dive magazines, and underwater film makers. I found there were only a few handful of men and women in the entire world professionally working in this career, and I was one of them. Suddenly the world seemed a whole lot smaller. But I am getting a little ahead of myself; let me tell you about our first shows we filmed.

Chapter 6

Our First Show

Show 1: *Beautiful Cozumel, the Drift-Diving Capital of the World* (Filmed in February 2005)

As with all our DVDs in the series, we created a box cover for each video, and the script on the back describes what each DVD is about. In this book, as we introduce you to each show, the box cover description will be specially spaced to set it apart from the general text. This one reads as follows:

> Cozumel is known for its rich Mayan heritage found throughout the island, but it is also famous to divers, who come here from all over the globe, because it is the drift-diving capital of the world. The island's dive shops can accommodate as many as eleven hundred divers a day, who go down under to check out the magical reefs in some of the warmest and clearest tropical water in the world. In this program from the *Dive Travel* video adventure series, we take you on a tour of the Caribbean Island, giving you a peek topside of the island's attractions (including San Miguel, the island's only town) as well as a typical week of diving on the ever-popular reefs surrounding Cozumel. See the spectacular and colorful coral reefs as they unfold before your eyes as well as the marine life only native here. Sit back and enjoy!

The first show we made was a return trip to Cozumel in February 2005 with my instructor, Morris. This time, however, with more experience under my belt and a new camera and housing system, that would become my first system to shoot with in the digital format, which had just arrived as the newest high-tech camera—long before HD. We shot only a total of the first six shows in this digital format. Being digital only is why they aren't included in our later Blu-ray production lineup, which requires high-definition technology.

What drift diving means to a scuba diver is this. You simply get in the water, go down with the group (led by a divemaster), and literally fly along with the currents. They carry you under the ocean along the reefs and among the marine life, with you hardly having to swim at all. Amazingly, you drift along the colorful corals and sea life with little exertion. The only drawback is that sometimes you move so fast in the current that it's hard to stop for any specialized photography shoots. It's the lazy man's way to dive, being carried along in a peaceful, relaxed state. Once you get out of the current, a dive boat simply picks you up at the surface with little effort.

All our shows offer a typical week of diving on the ever-popular, colorful coral reefs, which exist in each dive location, as well as the marine life native there. We found one thing in particular most divers like about our shows, unlike most island propaganda films highlighting things to see and do, which are filmed over many years to capture everything that ever visited or occurred on the island. We instead take a one-week tour, and what we film in that time frame is what you see, like any diver taking a one-week vacation there. This offers a more realistic view and approach to what you might see during a typical dive vacation. Interestingly enough, I have found that as many non-divers enjoy our shows as divers. When I show one of my films at a church group, for example, the people seem to enjoy seeing things not offered in any other venue. These people more than likely will never dive or venture across the planet, and they indicate that they especially like my narrative talk beforehand.

I talked to an older lady once, who worked for UPS and had never had an opportunity to travel or even take much vacation time. I used to see her when shipping off DVDs to various locations; she always asked about them. One day she seemed down in the dumps, and I offered her a DVD to watch, hoping it would cheer her up. She later told me she took it home and didn't watch it right away, but when she did, she said she was amazed and felt so relaxed while watching it. She said it made her feel like she was on vacation yet while never having to leave her rocking chair. I also toured the caves, caverns, and wreck of Cozumel, which would become show number two.

Show 2: *The Caves, Caverns, and Wreck of Cozumel* (Filmed in 2005)

Again, the box cover reads:

> In this show, we take you on an underwater, narrated excursion down to one hundred thirty-two feet through the famous caves and caverns located on the southern end of Cozumel Island. The Caribbean waters are crystal clear along the Grand Mayan Reef, the second longest barrier reef in the world. First, we tour the topside attractions, which draw as many as a dozen cruise ships at any one time to the famous Mexican port, class rated as the fifth most popular island in the world. Then we take you down dark and deep through the infamous Devil's Throat, a cave system that comes out at a depth of one hundred thirty feet, and tour other caves and caverns of Cozumel. The cave systems here are spectacular to see, and many are swim-through arches. We also tour through the island's only wreck, known as the *C53*, which was specifically sunk for divers. Hold on to your seats for this one!

I went back to Michigan with enough footage, both topside and underwater, to produce two separate half-hour shows. In the beginning, we made only half-hour shows. Later we expanded to an hour-long show to get in all the sights, both topside and underwater, which we videotaped around the islands. Both of these programs would become our first two video production shows, in what would eventually become a series called *Dive Travel*.

Show 3: *Key West, a Diving Adventure* (Filmed in April 2005)

> Ernest Hemingway lived, fished, and wrote on this island he called home. Join *Dive Travel*, a video adventure series, for its third released show in our series. An introduction to the show begins on the front lawn of the famous Hemingway house in Key West. Then come along with us as we dive the Atlantic Reef, America's only living coral reef. This one-hundred-fifty-mile system parallels the Keys, four to five miles offshore from Biscayne Bay to the Marquesas. We also take you to two of Key West's popular wrecks: *The Cayman Salvage Master* and *Joe's Tug*. But before we dive, we take you on a mystical tour of party town in Key West style, where you will observe the landmark at the southernmost point in the continental United States. Key West is the home to key lime pie, a naval base, exotic plants, natural coconut trees, almost thirty thousand year-round residents, and its free-roaming chickens.

Key West, a Diving Adventure in Florida became our third show in the series, again filmed in 2005. I was friends with a young computer guy and fellow dive buddy named Ty. We had taken many of the dive courses together that I mentioned earlier, including divemaster. Later we took a trip after receiving various dive certifications. Our very first and only dive trip together was to Key West, Florida. I had already been to Key West on three different occasions; the very first was with a dear friend, Bill, about my age, whose dad had recently died. We went down together for a week to simply get away, have fun, and kind of check out what the area had to offer. We went boating, parasailing, boat sailing, and just enjoying the Key West atmosphere.

We even went out on a catamaran, and I tried my first snorkel experience. I found it wasn't that great for me, but it was a real learning experience, making me realize I wasn't that much into snorkeling—bobbing around on the surface—but you have to try it to really know whether you like it. I didn't really like trying to breathe through a snorkel, and the limited viewing I got was just mostly from the surface, unless I could hold my breath long enough to stay down. I wanted to be down below. What I really wanted to do was take a dive lesson. We stopped by a local dive shop while in Key West to see whether they had a recreation course offering for a trial to see whether I liked it or not, but they were busy, so we went home. After thinking about it, I started getting serious about wanting to learn to dive.

A couple of years later, my dive buddy, Ty, and I (both recent divemaster graduates) went out diving with a dive shop in Key West and began filming our third show in the series: *Key West, a Diving Adventure*. Our shows are made into two sections: a topside of attractions to see from a non-diver point of view of what the island is all about preceded by a tour of Google Earth with a description of the city, country of origin, and a little history of the region. So the Key West video begins with me standing on the front lawn of the famous landmark, the Hemingway house, for my opening scene and introduction. We got permission from the house museum to use it. The museum is located at 907 Whitehead Street, across from the Key West Lighthouse close to the southern coast of the island. It is open daily to visitors. Ernest Hemingway was an American journalist, novelist, short-story writer, and sportsman. He arrived in April 1928 and lived in the house from 1931 to 1939. He wrote many of his works at this house.

Chapter 7

Travelogues

The basic concept of the show, *Dive Travel*, was a travelogue for scuba divers wishing to dive at various locations. The shows offer a diver what to expect to see on an island tour topside; then they take the diver on a tour below the ocean to check out the water clarity, marine life, reefs, and wrecks. They also give divers a basic overview of the area, so they can simply watch the show and decide whether they want to travel to that particular location. Since it costs a lot of money to travel and dive at various locations, the video is invaluable as an investment before spending money on a trip you might not enjoy.

On average, once I really got into producing the shows, I came back with about thirty-three hours of video from each dive location—half topside and half underwater. All were shot on mini video cassette tapes, which I had to download into the editing computer. I then began the editing process in our production studio. Over the years, I had three younger, computer-skilled guys: Ty, Eric, and Ben. One at a time, each taught me and helped me begin to build the show's base, with each show following a similar format. I had never edited before and wasn't even that educated on computers to begin with.

So the show threw me another learning curve, and it would take years to accomplish all I needed to know to produce a show. They said I would eventually learn how to edit, and I did after a while, all by trial and error. I can remember some days when I worked on editing many scenes, getting them just the way I wanted them, only to find I had forgotten to save my work. When I shut the computer down at the end of the day, I lost a day's work and had to start all over again the next day. Don't you just love computers? Had I had a window nearby, I think I might have thrown the computer out of it on more than one occasion. Prior to this, I had never had a computer of my own to utilize, let alone a second editing computer. So this was a totally new experience for me.

I was alone most of the time while writing scripts, producing audio, going through the many thirty-three hours of video, selecting each scene I wanted to use, and matching it to an audio track with interviews. Initially, I had to lay down a complete audio track from beginning to end of the show, including the music. Then I had to carefully edit and produce each show, which took an average of four months to complete. I pulled in each video clip, and there were well over a thousand clips per show, some only a second or two in length. I had to pull them all in one at a time by hand, making an hour-long video. Each hour consisted of hundreds and hundreds of actual edits.

Once I had all the editing done that I could do, the young guys came in and helped me with the final edits. I needed their expertise since I hadn't learned how to finalize and render the footage and produce a master of the final show on DVD. Then we had to print copies of the shows on DVD, burn a picture on the DVD, and produce a box, with its colorful artwork, to put it in. To create these box covers, I used Print Masters in Cadillac, Michigan; Gayle

Maurer, one of their graphic designers, helped me with the entire series. I gave her the copy and pictures, and she put them all together for each of the show's DVD covers to match up with the actual DVD we had produced. By now, it had become a full-scale production just to get the recording out. I had neighbors and even my grandchildren help in a production line to put the DVD boxes together with the cover on the front, place the DVD in the box, add a flyer inside, then shrink-wrap them for final distribution. The creative cover of the DVD showed both a topside and an underwater scene simultaneously, as if you were looking at the island and the underwater scene all at the same time. We used this same format for each of the shows we produced.

My plans were just to make a few shows to see how well they were received. I had no intention initially of producing as many as we ended up with. After all, this was supposed to be just a hobby following my retirement from the broadcasting industry. It eventually became a much bigger hobby than I ever expected.

Scuba divers overall have a super variety of diving interests. Some are into just diving on shipwrecks and exploring ships that have sunk to the bottom of the sea. These ships were either natural shipwrecks that sank in adverse weather or natural disasters in the ocean or on the Great Lakes, while other ships were purposely sunk to serve as artificial reefs for scuba divers to explore at various tropical locations as a diving sport. Sea ports like Key West, for example, make millions of dollars in revenue from divers who dive wrecks at each location. Communities even raise money to buy these vacant decommissioned ships and to have them sunk as artificial reefs for that reason alone due to the tourist dollars they generate. It costs a lot to obtain a ship from the government to be sunk as an artificial reef. They first must be cleaned from oil, grease, and environmental problems; and the inside doors are taken off as a safety precaution, costing sometimes millions of dollars just to prepare them to be sunk in the ocean.

Many divers are only into marine life exploration, along with following the excitement of filming or examining the over two hundred twenty-eight thousand (estimated at this writing) types of marine life species in our oceans. They enjoy whales, sharks, manta rays, and colorful fish, both large and small, closeup and personal. Still others are into the beautiful coral reefs and the over twenty-five hundred varieties of corals found around the world. Others are perhaps interested in drift diving, where the current propels them along without having to swim—they simply ride along for the fun of it. Some divers are into deep-water, technical diving, where they wear a variety of tanks and switch from tank to tank, breathing various gases as they descend to the deep areas, where normal recreational divers don't go.

Some scuba divers are into marine biology and the tagging of marine life to learn more about specific species and to document just how far marine life travel in our oceans. Amazingly, many sharks, for example, travel from country to country, spanning thousands of miles as their backyard.

There are many divers like me who are into underwater photography. Even that category is broken into two sub-categories: those who enjoy only still photography and others who are into videography. There are so many different types of scuba diving activities that one could never get tired of the diving experience. Some diving enthusiasts are into just diving local rivers, freshwater lakes, or the Great Lakes, with no real interest in the ocean whatsoever. Many others are into treasure hunting, looking for sunken treasure, maybe something that sank to the bottom of a lake, like an outboard motor or anchor. Of course, there are also real treasure hunters worldwide who professionally seek out ships for their lost treasure such as pirate ships containing gold, coins, and historical artifacts. Then finally there are those much-needed and respected search and rescue divers who, often in horrible dive conditions, such as hard currents and dark cloudy water, search for bodies from drowning mishaps or perhaps for criminal weapons tossed into rivers or lakes.

Chapter 8

My Last Breath of Air

Show 4: *Key Largo and the Upper Keys of Florida, a Diving Destination* (Filmed in April 2005)

In this *Dive Travel* adventure series, we take you to the sky with a helicopter ride over Key Largo, the northernmost island of the Florida keys island chain, and fly over Molasses Reef, one of the many reefs just offshore. Our diving tour of the Upper Keys begins with a stop at Marathon Key, where we visit the *Thunderbolt* wreck and area reefs. Then we are on to Islamorada, known as the sport-fishing capital of the world, where we dive the *Eagle* wreck. In Key Largo, the diving capital, we visit the Christ of the Abyss underwater bronze statue in the John Pennekamp Coral Reef Preserve. While in Key Largo, we also dive the gigantic five-hundrd-ten-foot *Spiegel Grove*, the largest artificial reef site in the United States at the time. On our last day of diving, we take you on a shark feed, where we encounter several nurse sharks, a two hundred fifty pound goliath grouper, and a barracuda. Join us for the fun!

Our fourth show we produced was *Key Largo and the Upper Keys of Florida, a Diving Destination*. We shot the video for it while Ty and I were in Florida in April 2005, producing the Key West show. So we came back with two more shows to work on. Suddenly, I had four shows, all backed up in the computer, to begin work on.

It was here that, unbeknownst to me, my diving might very well have come to an end with my own death! It would be the only time in my entire diving experience that this thought crossed my mind. Luckily, I survived all my future dives, but this one was a scary experience for me.

We had gone down and filmed the shipwreck. It was an early-morning dive and my very first dive of the day. Everything was going great while filming the ship below until I started to go up the tagline rope we had descended earlier. It went down to the ship and was attached to a big buoy at the surface. I was hanging on the rope doing my three-minute safety stop. We are all required to do a safety stop following the dive, just as others below me were doing at the fifteen-feet interval. The purpose is to help off-gas the nitrogen absorbed while diving. It helps to unload nitrogen and give the body time to release that nitrogen slowly.

The waves on the surface above were very rough at the time. The rope was going up and down in a washing machine fashion, and high waves were bashing the buoy on the surface. When we had descended earlier that morning, things were calm with minimal wave action. But by the time we were coming up, a storm was brewing, and waves were starting to build on the surface. Sometimes at sea storms seem to come out of nowhere, and divers and deckhands on ships can get into immediate danger.

Trying to hold onto the rope with my big camera system weighing thirty-eight pounds was always a challenge, let alone having to be thrown about like a ragdoll hanging onto this heavy rope tagline to the ship. Suddenly, I took a breath of air from my regulator, and instead of air, I got a mouthful of salt water. My mind raced and instantly went into shock, thinking, *How could this happen*? I had my mouthpiece in my mouth, nothing seemed abnormal, and yet I wasn't breathing air any longer. In my training as a divemaster, they had always stressed, *Don't ever panic! Think things through and analyze carefully the situation at hand.* Obviously, *whoever wrote the book on that was never suddenly thrust into my predicament,* or so I thought at the time.

I took a second breath just to make sure I hadn't somehow mistakenly used my mouthpiece, only to find the same thing happen as nasty salt water came in, and again, I had no air. The moment lasted only seconds, but it seemed like a long time, with my mind so delirious with the thought of dying. I knew that if I stayed there, I was going to die from the lack of oxygen. I had also been told in training that if I got into a life-saving problem, I should drop my camera and let it go. Instead, I should save myself or the one I was with. The camera could be replaced but not a human life. The only other option was to go to one's dive buddy and grab his or her spare octopus mounted on the front of his or her BCD, which each of us was required to carry. Unfortunately, no one was close to me to do that, and I was running out of time.

Well, I decided I wasn't about to let go of my very expensive camera system, since I was already near the surface. The dark and cloudy bottom lay over one hundred feet below me. I didn't know whether I could even reach the surface without air in my lungs. I was still fifteen feet below the surface at this time, and I could no longer breathe. I had taken my last breath seconds ago. All I sensed was that if I didn't break free, I would die right there.

They say when you are about to die, thoughts of your life flash before you. Well, a lot raced through my mind in that instant. I worried about what my family would think if told I had died on a dive under the ocean as a new diver. I would never see any of my grandchildren again. I asked God right then to help me get to the boat safely. While the event seemed like a very long time, it was only less than a minute.

Struggling, I made a jump for it, letting go of the buoy tagline, and swam to the surface. Finally reaching the surface safely, now I had another worry. I bobbed up near the buoy and near the dive boat, somewhat relieved and yet worried that by not completing my safety stop, I might be in danger of getting the bends or having to go to a decompression chamber. A decompression or hyperbaric chamber allows surface-supplied-gas divers to complete their decompression stops in a chamber rather than underwater. Few are readily available; usually a diver must be transported to one in a larger city that has one. I had been on a deep dive over one hundred foot or more. Had it been the second or third dive of the day, I might have been in trouble.

I told the boat captain upon surfacing what had happened, and he said I would be fine. Since it was the first dive of the day, it was okay to miss the safety stop. I thanked God and was relieved I had made it safely back on the boat. I was a relatively new diver, so I still had a lot of experience yet to gain.

After the captain of the boat checked over my system, we found the mystery as to what had happened to me. He said it had been a bizarre accident, that my regulator mouthpiece had come unattached from the air hose dangling behind me, which I had never once noticed or heard bubbling overhead. That was why I was sucking in salt water instead of air.

Oh my, I thought, *no wonder!* That rough surge of the rope had yanked the hose off my mouthpiece. The simple solution to correcting that problem—now with time to think things through, had I known what happened—was to simply drop that mouthpiece and take my spare regulator mouthpiece, which is referred to as an "octopus" mounted in front of me, and use it instead, since it was still attached. Then I would have been just fine. But the confusion resulted from my not being able to see what had happened. My thoughts were that my tank could have been empty of air even though the computer said I was fine. All I understood at the time, which amounted to a mere few seconds, was that I was going to die without air. This was a life lesson for me and a wake-up call to understand in the future.

Can you imagine that happening to you one hundred feet below the surface while at a shipwreck? Like our training instructor said, "Don't panic!" Had I seen my air hose come unattached behind me, I would have been able to mentally resolve the problem by myself while still hanging on to the rope. Since that time, I have come to assist others who were under the ocean and out of air; they came to get my spare octopus to breathe on as we both headed for the surface. But my first experience of thinking I was going to die was something I would long remember. As a new diver, I remember starting out being very naïve, like most divers are, but with experience and seasoned dives under my belt, I eventually became more aware of my surroundings.

Continuing our dive in Key Largo, we visited the Christ of the Abyss underwater statue in the John Pennekamp Coral Reef Preserve. While in Key largo, we dove the largest, artificial reef site in the USA. At the time we filmed the gigantic, five-hundred-ten-foot *Spiegel Grove*.

Here's an interesting footnote to the story about the sinking of the *Spiegel Grove*, which was sunk to be an artificial reef. When it was originally sunk, it landed on its side rather than in an upright position as anticipated. But after much research, the team that sank it and area scuba clubs were in the process of raising a couple of million dollars to have it lifted and straightened up so it would stand upright on the ocean floor. But before they could accomplish that feat, Mother Nature came along in the form of a hurricane and automatically put the ship on course, setting her perfectly upright as they had anticipated. It is another wonder of nature. Who would have thought hurricanes with such powerful winds could upright a heavy ship, sitting in water hundreds of feet deep?

Hurricanes have, however, played that same course on many ships in the past, sometimes even destroying them deep in the depths of the oceans. Mother Nature not only controls what you see on the earth's surface but also plays either some havoc or an important role under the oceans of the planet. Storms like that can destroy reefs by covering them with sand and smothering the reef system until it eventually dies.

We had a successful dive that day, filming the *Spiegel Grove*'s outer decks and getting footage to use for the show, but we didn't enter the ship. Just a few years later, three trained, technical divers educated in deep dives entered the *Spiegel Grove* and never came out. They reportedly went to the back of the ship and supposedly got lost from all the silt inside the ship; they couldn't find their way out to safety and died in one of the passageways in the ship's lower levels. I now understand how frightening it would be to be trapped below and run out of air, knowing you will never make it out of the ship in time. What fearful thoughts one must be thinking at that time. The only thing left to do is to pray to God.

Such tragedy happens occasionally to those divers who fail to use proper safety precautions when diving; they think they are invincible. This scenario occurs more often than you might think in other shipwrecks around the world as well as in deep cave systems and in other areas of the oceans, which are awaiting the entrapment of divers. The oceans can sometimes be a cruel reminder that adventurous discoveries below the surface sometimes come with a price.

Chapter 9

God Chose the Perfect Psalm

If I wasn't already busy enough, Morris invited me on a fifth film shoot to Bonaire. Part of the Netherlands Antilles (the ABC islands), it is made up of Aruba, Bonaire, and Curaçao, two of which I would visit in future shows.

Show 5: *Bonaire, a Tropical Desert Island* (Filmed in June 2005)

> Bonaire is part of the Netherlands Antilles, made up of Aruba, Curaçao, and Bonaire. It lies fifty miles north of Venezuela, outside the Caribbean hurricane belt. It is well known among divers to be the shore-diving capital of the world. Drive around the island, and you will find the reef locations marked with yellow and painted stones along parking areas. Swim out a few yards, and you can dive 24/7 into the crystal-clear waters and see the beautiful, colorful reefs that surround the island. Dive Travel takes you on a week's safari topside. Tour the back country, salt industry, and the ancient slave huts. See the wild donkeys, flamingoes, and native lizards. Then join us as we dive the reefs and discover the marine life that inhabits the clear, warm waters of the Caribbean. Lac Bay is also a premier, world-class windsurfing destination, rated by Windsurfing Magazine as the number one place to learn and improve your windsurfing skills!

While on the island getting topside video, I came across a mural displaying a Bible verse; it blew me away the minute I saw it. I was so excited after seeing it that I decided the Bible verse must be the lead-in for each show. We were driving around the island and came upon a big billboard; the entire side of the billboard had a color mural painted on it of a beautiful reef system complete with marine life. At the bottom of the mural in large letters was Psalm 107:24. "See the works of the Lord and his wonders in the deep."

Wow! I thought. *That is the most perfect scripture to fit my dive shows; it is better than anything I could ever come up with from the Bible on my own. Praise God!* God and God alone had shown me at that moment what was to be His signature logo to put at the beginning of each of my *Dive Travel* shows—a tribute to our God for His wondrous works from the depths of the ocean below. The full Psalm leading up to it in the King James Version is Psalm 107:23–24. "They that go down to the sea in ships, that do business in great waters; These see the works of the Lord, and his wonders in the deep." I got the verse just in time, too, to properly insert it in front of our very first finished show in the series, and it continues at the beginning of each show and throughout the entire thirty-seven-volume series.

We visited Bonaire with a group of divers from the local dive shop in Cadillac. This island allows divers to dive off the beaches and not have to employ boats to take them out diving.

I hadn't been on many night dives, and the group wanted to do a night dive each evening after diving all day. Why not a fourth or fifth dive of the day? We had nothing else to do. Well, for those of you who are afraid of the dark, especially in water, this is probably not for you. You suit up at just about dusk and go down under the ocean with search lights or in my case lights on my underwater housing that would last, at best, maybe forty-five minutes before running off batteries. This way you can see some of the night-time attractions. If my camera lights went out from a depleted battery, I had a spare underwater flashlight with me.

There under the deep, dark water were many nocturnal marine species, such as octopus, crabs, eels, and sharks. They hunt at night while other fish are in their sleep mode. When darkness arrives, many of the creatures hiding during the day come out to party at night. These nocturnal hunters were out and about on the ocean floor and swimming over reefs in search of a nighttime snack. It is mostly the only time they are active, especially octopuses. It is the one time of day you can almost guarantee seeing one; that is why night dives are so popular with divers.

With the emerging darkness in front of you, except for what your flashlight shows you, it is like going down a dark alley at night and wondering just what is going to instantly jump out at you or startle you into wanting to wet your already-wet suit. Some define it as a Halloween nightmare on steroids. You keep watching the shadows surrounding you, causing your mind to think something is following you in the darkness. Like where things go bump in the night!

Can you tell I totally like this nighttime activity? Fortunately, or unfortunately, there seems to be night diving every night. Had I been alone, I wouldn't have gone, but with a group of divers, it is a group thing to do. On this night, I came upon a brown moray eel in search of dinner. Suddenly, I caught him in my lights on camera; he was quickly swimming along the reef and peeking into various coral holes, looking for other easy sea life to eat. Then he finally attacked a green parrot fish, which was hiding in the reef. Instantly, the dirt rolled off the sand bar reef. He had latched onto a fish that couldn't escape its jaws.

I thought, *I wouldn't like to be a fish trying to sleep at night on a reef after dark, just waiting there and having to worry about being eaten alive.* What a night life these poor sleepers in the deep have. It was fun, however, to see the various fish species just kind of hanging out in a sleep mode and trying to avoid our bright lights, which hovered over the reef. It was common to see turtles resting for the night inside a big barrel sponge. I couldn't blame them. I think I would hide too.

Other things that made swimming in the dark of night somewhat scary were those very large tarpon, which were several feet in length. Some, fairly large in girth, suddenly appeared out of nowhere and swam right over our shoulders, following our search lights in search of smaller fish lying on the reef system. If our lights shined on one of the smaller fish, the tarpon attacked it. They had become accustomed to night divers with lights and were cheating the hunting system by our lighting their way to prey. To protect some of the fish, we had to be careful not to shine a light on them for too long, or we would be spotlighting their death.

I can remember a woman one night who immediately swam to the surface, screaming, "Shark! Shark!" But it was only a rather large tarpon swimming over her shoulder, but it was enough to frighten the unsuspecting diver nearly to death. This was just one of my many night dives, since every dive location around the world offered them to those who weren't afraid to go under the water at night. On liveaboard boats, it was a typical night entertainment attraction for scuba divers to always night dive into the dark depths of the sea.

We had a strange thing happen to us on one of these night dives while surfacing. One of our divers got stung from what we believed to be a box jellyfish. He was stung just as we surfaced under the lights at the dock. Jellyfish often come to the surface at night while attracted to the lights. We ended up taking the diver to the emergency room. He was in bad shape soon after it happened. Box jellies are dangerous. I was sitting next to him in the back seat of the vehicle, trying to keep him awake. I was afraid he was going to pass out on the way to the hospital. After some prolonged treatment, which seemed like hours had gone by, he was released, though somewhat groggy, for us to take him back to the hotel. He was my roommate, so I laid awake all night, afraid he might not make it. But by the next morning, he was miraculously fine, and after a good breakfast, he was ready to go diving again. I have to say he was better off than I was.

On another night in Bonaire, we had rented a small pickup truck to drive around the island to hold our tanks and diving gear. We had just filled it with gas and drove out to one of the many reefs located far away at the end of the island to shore-dive just before dark again as a night dive. We parked the vehicle. One of our divers left some of his jewelry inside the truck, and when we returned to the truck, we found the vehicle had been robbed. The culprits had also siphoned all our gas from the tank, leaving us with only fumes to drive back on. Fortunately, we made it back, but to add insult to injury, we found out when turning in the rented vehicle that the thieves had even stolen a spare tire mounted under the truck. We didn't even know it was there, but the rental company made us pay for it. We suspected that it was an inside job.

In addition to the diving, we also took a safari tour of Bonaire Island in our truck, touring the harsh, rough cactus and scrub-brush back country. The salt industry on the island was impressive with huge, high piles of white sea salt. Here they pumped ocean water into pools on land, then let them settle and dry. Finally, they scooped up the ocean salt and, with the help of an elevator, poured the salt into giant mountains of salt for storage. These mountains were visible from most any location on the island. At certain times, when cargo ships arrived, they loaded the salt onto the ships bound for destinations around the world, to be sold as sea salt.

We also toured the ancient slave huts and saw wild donkeys, flamingoes, and native lizards on this edition of *Dive Travel*. Plus, we saw Lac Bay, a premier, world-class windsurfing destination. *Windsurfing Magazine* rated this location as the number one place to learn and improve windsurfing skills. All in all, it was an impressive island.

Morris, my dive instructor, and me producing a show just off the coast in Bonaire

Chapter 10

Belize, My First Liveaboard Adventure

Last but not least, show number six, our final show to be filmed in digital video, was a trip I took with another dive buddy to the country of Belize.

Show 6: *Belize, Home of the Famous Blue Hole* (Filmed in October 2005)

Belize is known for its ancient Maya Ruins, beautiful rain forest, magnificent barrier reef, and wonderful miles of cave system. On this show, my dive buddy and I take a trip on a liveaboard ship, the *Belize Aggressor*, forty-five miles off the coast of Belize to Lighthouse Reef Atoll, one of four coral atolls in the Caribbean—home to two World Heritage sites: Half Moon Caye and Blue Hole National Monument, both managed by the Belize Audubon Society. Half Moon Caye is home to the red-footed booby bird. The Blue Hole was first made famous by Jacque Cousteau in the early '70s and has since become one of the most popular dive destinations in the world. Our Belize topside adventure takes you on a tour of Belize City, then an excursion of the rain forest jungles, home to the black howler monkeys and other native animals. We tour Altun Ha (Water of the Rock) Maya Ruins and get wet cave tubing through two of over seven miles of underground caves.

The blue hole is over four hundred feet deep—far beyond the scope for a recreational diver to reach—but it was fun anyway to see the stalactites deep inside. This was once a cave, and the top of the cave fell in, making it now just one gigantic hole above the cave. It is a spectacular site from the air above it. It was all made of rock with little or no coral present. We were lucky to see it on a liveaboard boat, traveling around it for days. Some divers wanting to see it from shore needed to travel out over four hours just to see it and then go back. Many said it wasn't worth all the hype for the time it took to simply get out to it in the middle of the ocean. We were told Jacque Cousteau and his crew had blown out part of the circular hole to get his long ship inside to spend time examining the hole and its depths. Today, no one would ever be given permission to do such a thing, with this being a national monument.

Our Belize topside adventure takes you on a tour of the city, then an excursion of the rain forest jungles, home to the black howler monkeys and other native animals. The black howler monkey is known as the "baboon" in Belize. It is the largest monkey in Belize and one the largest in the Americas. There are at least six different species. They are also the noisiest animal in the Belize jungle, and they can be heard up to a mile away. The black howler monkey is about two to three feet in length and weighs about fifteen pounds. They live in Central and South American rain forests. The canopy layer of the rain forest is their home, although you will see them spend a lot of time on the ground as well. They eat mainly fruits and nuts. The monkeys love to irritate jaguars from high up in the canopy, sometimes even throwing sticks and branches at the jaguar below. Howler monkeys "wake up" the rain forest in the morning and "sing it to sleep" at night, sometimes even singing just before it rains. They live in troops of four to ten or more members, depending on the species. Howlers are good swimmers, have excellent vision, and can see up to a half mile away. Their lifespan is about twenty years.

We had these wild monkeys trying to climb our legs and looking for the bananas we were holding to feed them, and they were eating bananas out of our hands. Natives escorted us through the back jungles to see these primates, which we videotaped during our adventure. You will enjoy watching them in the Belize show.

When we were in Belize, we noticed a lot of military guards stationed everywhere in the downtown area, which made us feel a little uncomfortable at times. We were told not to go downtown at night.

I found it fascinating to watch the leaf-cutting ants carry leaves across the jungle track. I could have watched them for hours, each carrying a heavy leaf in its mouth like a parade in a caravan heading back to its home. Also, in the show, we toured Altun Ha (water of the rock) Maya Ruins and got wet while cave-tubing through two of the over seven miles of underground caves. These caves were amazing inside and out, and we floated inside the caves in waist-deep water using headlights mounted on our helmets to see the stalactites hanging down low from the ceilings of the caves, which were dark in many areas. These caves were incredible, and they went on for miles inside this extremely long cave system, with the rivers carrying us along in our inner tubes as we traveled by floating down a river through the caves. This was one of my very first experiences to dive off a liveaboard boat, but it wouldn't be my last. Over the years, I had been on over a dozen such ships that ply the oceans, offering diving 24/7 as they traverse the oceans and seas of the world.

I preferred diving and filming to sitting back at the office and editing. I had to go through thirty-three or more hours of video I traditionally shot at each location I attended. It was always a job to search out the segments we wanted to use, but since I was the one who filmed it, I am the only one who knew what footage to use and where to find each scene. Therefore, it was the necessary thing I alone had to do. I videotaped every scene, both topside and under the ocean as a videographer, seeing to it that my camera equipment and all my dive gear and suitcases arrived safely at each location. I was exceedingly careful to carry it with me everywhere, from the time I got off the plane to the time I departed for home.

Once at home, we had to surf through all the filmed footage, selecting the scenes, writing the scripts, selecting the music, laying the soundtrack, then slowly and tirelessly editing each video clip to match what the soundtrack called for. Finally, and only in the very end, I received some help in finalizing the show to render it, and at last, I turned it into a completed DVD. I guess that is why I am so proud of the series today. I put so much effort into telling a story from each location to make divers want to go there and see for themselves the adventure I had just spent time showing them. These were, after all, travelogues for divers to look at and decide whether this location was where they wanted to go for their next dive vacation. God has always taken care of me, kept me safe, and brought me back home alive. Praise be to Him.

Chapter 11

My Prayer

What started out as a hobby was becoming real work at the editing station back home, while filming on location was more like being on vacation. Belize was filmed in October 2005. Now I had six shows in the lineup, and we hadn't even completed show number one editing wise. I had to seriously get to work at home. *No more diving for a while.* Or so I thought.

Things were starting to take off, so it was time to go to the Lord in prayer. My prayer to Jesus was that if this was what He indeed wanted me to do in the second part of my life, then I would pray that God would just keep me safe in filming His magnificent oceans and seas with His wonders in the deep around the world. I in turn would be eternally blessed and grateful to show the world His beautiful creations as described in Genesis. I would include all His many works from the deep: the colorful corals, His majestic marine life, the mountains, and caves—all I had captured in my travels on video. I would make it available to as many people as I could by making underwater shows from many locations around the world. I would show them at churches, youth groups, schools, community fundraisers, and wherever anyone would invite me to come and educate them on God's underwater creations.

My favorite verse in the Bible is all about the "fifth day" of God's creation. Genesis 1:20–23 says, "And God said, Let the waters bring forth abundantly the moving creature that hath life, and fowl that may fly above the earth in the open firmament of heaven. And God created great whales, and every living creature that moveth, which the waters brought forth abundantly, after their kind, and every winged fowl after his kind: and God saw that it was good. And God blessed them, saying, 'Be fruitful and multiply, and fill the waters in the seas, and let fowl multiply in the earth. And the evening and the morning were the fifth day."

Most people never get a chance to even begin to understand what God's amazing creations look like below the deep. If you look at all the variety of marine life under the sea—all in spectacular colors and designs—you can see for yourself that each fish had a creative designer to make it special like we are.

Having seen the world around me from above and underwater, I believe God created everything, just as His word says in Genesis, and we are all accountable to the creator of life. I am a believer in the Bible and how God created life in the beginning with Adam and Eve with the first breath of life. We cannot be born from rocks; we need DNA and a design so intricate that only a God could create it. Just look at the intricate design of the human body alone. Well, each fish is as different and unique from the other as we are. I really have a passion for diving and filming and wanting to show others just how awesome that world down deep below the oceans really looks. Especially for those of you who have a fear of water but still have interest in, and are intrigued by, as well as curious about what it must look like below.

After praying and talking to God and making my promise to Him, suddenly it was like I was blessed. The whole world just seemed to open up. Previously, I had paid for most of my own trips while getting started abroad. Now many dive shops and places around the world invited me to visit their exotic ports of the world as hosts. Some paid only for my diving and hotel accommodations, while at their location, which was a start, while others picked up my entire roundtrip airfare as well. I suddenly had more trips than I could handle. So be prepared and be careful what you pray for; sometimes God blesses you in more ways than you might expect. Yes, God is good!

My dive shop alerted me in 2006 that I was invited to represent the dive shop on a trip to Fiji with another group of divers from all over the country on a guided, free tour. It was free since our host over in Fiji wanted to show us the many diving opportunities and attractions there, so dive shops would offer more trips to Fiji. Our group was made up of journalists and dive shop owners looking to find out what diving was like in Fiji so they could go back home and sell trips there. Otherwise it would be referred to as a marketing trip by future dive shops. I first had to fly to Los Angeles, but then I joined a group of divers on a special trip to Fiji aboard Pacific Airlines. I had just purchased a new camera from Sony and a new housing from Gates Underwater Housings, who produced one of the best systems in the underwater housing world at the time. I had a new lighting system for it, and I was all excited to film, finally in HD widescreen, in a country that was known for its multi-colorful, soft corals. I thought, *Wow! What a way to launch our newest show in HD!*

I arrived in Los Angeles for the trip but had counted the time wrong somehow and missed the plane that had left a day earlier. I called the travel company that had arranged it, and they said I could still come on the next flight, but Pacific Airlines flew on only certain days of the week, so I had to wait a couple of more days and then fly over and join the tour in progress. I was slightly embarrassed, but I got to tour the *NAIA*, a sailing vessel that had already taken the group out to sea for the first three days of the trip.

All I got was a tour of the ship upon its arrival back at port but then got to continue with the tour. The only good part was that since I had missed the first three days, I got to stay on the island a few extended days longer, going out on my own after the others had left for home. It was on those final days that I found the best diving of the entire week-long trip. So I guess maybe it was good I was late; God had saved the best diving for me, and me alone, at another location on the far side of the island. I often tend to underestimate how God is far ahead of our individual thinking, because He has planned our lives for us. He is in control; we just need to trust the Lord daily.

Show 7: *Fiji* (Filmed in March 2006)

Fiji, the home of tropical South Pacific Islands, became show number seven in our lineup and our first show to be filmed in HD widescreen with a super, wide-angle lens.

> As Fiji natives say, "Bula" or "Welcome to Fiji." This country is truly one of the friendliest on earth, considering that in 1789 it was well known to a cautious Captain William Bligh and passing ships as the land of cannibals. Fiji is richly made up of over three hundred thirty-three beautiful, exotic tropical islands in the South Pacific. There we visit four different dive destinations, all off the main island of Viti Levu. We dive the reefs off Wananavu, where we see vibrant multicolored soft corals and over twelve hundred species of fish. We visit a native Fijian village for a ceremonial dance and are served their native drink, "Kava," in a somewhat religious ceremony much like communion, by the local villagers. It is all done one person at a time while sitting in a big circle. After a walk through

the jungle and a swim at a heart-shaped pool and a waterfall, which comes down from the rain forest and mountains above, we are on to tour the *NAIA*, a Fiji liveaboard boat. Later, we travel by water taxi to a nearby island, known as Castaway Island, and tour their resort across from a small, uninhabited island where Tom Hanks made his famous movie *Castaway*. Here we dive the reefs and view the marine life living there, such as lionfish and blue-ribbon eels. Then we visit the famous Beqa Lagoon, where we go on an exciting shark-feeding adventure. Join us for our helicopter tour of the dense rain forest and jungles with magnificent cascading waterfalls in this picturesque country only Fiji can provide. "Vinaka" ("Thank you"). Sit back and enjoy one of *Dive Travel's* most exotic locations ever and the very first show in our series shot exclusively in HD widescreen.

Some of the most beautiful healthy reefs in Beqa Lagoon, Fiji

A funny thought crossed my mind at the airport when I first arrived. I laughed when I saw a tourist's T-shirt with these words printed on it: "Welcome to Fiji, we like to have you for lunch!" The Fijian people always greeted us on each island by singing a welcome song and by singing a farewell song a few days later on departure. Soon I was saying goodbye to the group I had traveled with as they prepared to head back to LA. They were all somewhat envious I got to stay on. I traveled alone on a bus over to the other side of the island to Beqa Lagoon and stayed at the Pearl Resort. The next day, I found what I refer to as God's underwater flower garden. The reefs are primarily made up of gorgeous, colorful, soft corals that sway in the current like leaves on a tree. I was totally mesmerized as I swam over and over the coral reefs, showing the most beautiful colors I have ever witnessed—all colors of the rainbow. But that isn't all; on top of the beautiful flower gardens, millions of colorful fish came out of the corals, adding a multitude of colors of every fish species imaginable. Another day I went on a shark feed and learned about why the dive shop fed the sharks there. By feeding the sharks, they built a greater habitat and reef structure.

God's underwater, colorful flower garden reefs in Beqa Lagoon, Fiji

Before I left, I took a helicopter tour of the area. I love riding and filming out of helicopters. I had flown before in planes, but it's just not the same. They go too fast, and it's hard to film out of the little windows. But in helicopters I learned pilots can take you to places no others can. I had a helicopter pilot ask me once, "What way do you want to fly over?" When I told him, he simply turned the helicopter around so my window or open door faced the exact area I wanted to film. This made it so easy to film. Suddenly I was a spoiled, flying videographer able to obtain most any video angle I desired.

Many times in exotic areas, I asked if the side passenger door could be removed for a better filming experience without having to shoot through a window, which was often dirty or tinted. Seat belts held us in place, so leaning out wasn't an issue. Fiji was no exception; after arriving at the airport, they were happy to take off the door for me with little effort, and soon we were in the air, filming over the beautiful tropical islands, surrounded by crystal, white-sand beaches. Corals surrounded the small islands with a mixture of the blue oceans and turquoise seas. We even flew up into the mountains and into the majestic rain forest, where it was raining when we arrived. I was constantly wiping my lens, and it was raining into where I was sitting while leaning out over the view below. Oh well. It was my idea to remove the door!

I was filming cascading waterfalls, shooting out of the side of the mountains; the waterfalls cascaded into streams and rivers, then ran down into the lush, green rain forest below. Over the years, I have filmed from dozens of helicopters, and this still is the best machine I have found to film from to get that "perfect as it gets" birds-eye view of the island or country below. But this was the only time I ever filmed in a real rain forest while it was indeed raining. "Vinaka (thank you), Fiji, for another great show!"

Chapter 12

The Blu-ray Dilemma

When I returned from Fiji, we were going to turn this show into our first HD widescreen production and attempt to make our first Blu-ray disc for our master after we had made another master on regular DVD. We had been making only regular DVDs up until now. But now it would take even longer. We would first have to make a regular DVD of the show, then re-render it in high definition and make a Blu-ray version of the same disc to release on Blu-ray. Henceforth, we would be making two separate DVDs of all our future shows, a regular for those who only had regular DVD players and a Blu-ray copy for those with the new Blu-ray disc players, which were just coming on the market for consumers. These were regarded as the best quality available in high-definition, widescreen video.

That process would become another learning curve for us. At the time, we could buy Blu-ray discs, which cost $21 each just for the blank ones only because it was the latest technology, and few were available. Today Blu-ray blanks cost less than fifty cents each. After we made our first copy of what we believed to be a Blu-ray disc, we took it into our local ABC warehouse, a retail store, to try to play it on one of their new Blu-ray players on display. We found it played on one player but not on a second player. We did the same at Best Buy with both Sony Blu-ray players, which had just come out on the market, as well as other brands like Samsung. Some played our first test show; others would not.

We called Sony's high-tech office in San Diego, California, and talked with them about our problem, asking why the Blu-ray discs played on some machines but not on others. They asked us to ship them a copy, and we did so for them to examine it. Later they called and told us they were surprised we had successfully produced a Blu-ray copy and that it was perfect. He told us he was impressed with our small company and said he thought we were one of the first small, independent companies that had ever produced a Blu-ray disc successfully.

That news made us feel proud, but what they said next made me wonder what we were getting ourselves into. They told us not all Blu-ray players were set to play what they termed "third-generation production," meaning those blank copies they sold. Their first Blu-ray players on the market were programmed to play only first-generation Hollywood movies. To play the copies we had just made, they instructed us to go online with our Blu-ray player and do an upgrade on the player itself to get it to play the disc. He informed us that each player was a miniature computer in itself and that by connecting players online, they could be reprogrammed. So after becoming frustrated on the phone with the tech, I asked him, "Do you mean to tell me that you are selling me a twenty-one-dollar blank Sony disc that won't even play in your own Sony Blu-ray players?" He laughed and said that yes, it was true—until we did the upgrades.

Having had a television background and having been a keen marketer in the past, with my experience in television, I thought, *What a marketing nightmare this may be—to make Blu-ray discs of the dive series people won't even be able to play. Worse yet, they will send them back to us, saying they aren't any good when they are perfectly good master Blu-ray discs.* I foresaw the problem as number one. To begin with, how would people know they had to do an upgrade on their brand-new player to play one of our products? Number two, how would they know what to do to accomplish this feat? It proved to be a problem for some in the beginning for sure, for people would call and say the disc wouldn't play on the new Blu-ray player they had just purchased. We tried to explain to them what to do, but they were confused. They said, "Well, it plays the movies we buy just fine but not your disc." It was as if ours were inferior. I finally had them send the disc back, offering them a refund or our shows on regular DVDs. Upon receiving it, I found, as I expected, that it played perfectly in our players at work. On our website, we tried to explain the dilemma and placed copies of what to do with each Blu-ray DVD sold; it seemed to help. Years later all Blu-ray players sold automatically had this upgrade built into them. But we were one of the first small, experimental companies to be on the cutting edge of technology. Sometimes, though, being on top of technology has its shortfalls.

I was at a national trade show for the scuba diving industry, called DEMA (Diving Equipment and Marketing Association). The show is held annually in Las Vegas one year and in Orlando the next, rotating locations every other year. It was at one of these shows that I was invited to join a shark-diving group of divers made up of many photojournalists, magazine and television photographers, and so forth. The group was destined to go to Guadalupe Island in Mexico, which became the next show in our *Dive Travel* lineup: *The Great White Sharks of Guadeloupe Island, Mexico.*

Chapter 13

Shark Education

I have heard guys say many times, "Why not kill all the sharks in the ocean? What do we need them for anyway?" This talk used to frustrate me to no end due to their lack of knowledge and ignorance. What most people don't understand is that without sharks in our ecosystem, we wouldn't eat as many fish as we currently do. Eliminating sharks would come to later harm the fisheries industry and even the corals around the world; they would suffer and die due to being unprotected by sharks. I will explain and later prove these comments to you. God put sharks and other fish in the ocean for a purpose, just as He put lions, bears, and elephants on the earth's surface for a reason. Each contributes to the ecosystem in its own special way.

Sharks are even more valuable. Sharks are the great policemen under the ocean; that is why the oceans need sharks. They tend to keep all marine life in check. For instance, I always use this example when talking to a group. When you are driving down a highway and spot a police car sitting alongside the road, you may notice how people tend to immediately slow down. Or they at least try to drive more carefully. Well, fish respond the same way when they see sharks approaching and patrolling a reef. They are just as afraid of sharks as humans are. I used to stand by a long reef system and watch sharks swim down the entire length until they were almost out of sight, only to patrol all the way back again.

Sharks have been swimming and patrolling the world's oceans for thousands of years. But today shark populations are being decimated by commercial fishing, putting some species in danger of extinction. On many dives I have been on with older divers, they said they used to see many more sharks on reefs below the ocean, but today it is a rare event to even come across one unless you are on a shark feed, and only then they come in for the bait offered by the dive shop. Sharks have unfortunately fallen victim to the man-hungry stereotype society has created for them. However, what the world should really fear is a world without sharks.

The reality is that humans are the true predators of the sea. Each year humans around the world kill more than one hundred million sharks in shark-finning industries, while sharks mistakenly kill only between five and twelve people annually out of the seven and a half billion humans on the planet. I find it strange, though, when a shark kills another human; the event is immediately in news headlines around the world, proclaiming that a shark killed a man. Why? Because of what I call the "*Jaws* syndrome."

Sharks are big news. Ever since the movie *Jaws* came out, any stories of shark attacks sell newspapers. It is interesting that Peter Benchley, who wrote the novel, which was later turned into the movie, was quoted as saying, "Had I known the repercussion sharks would be subjected too, after the movie came out, I would never have written that book." Following the movie, sharks were hunted down and killed at random all over the world as worthless critters; the world was scared to death of sharks living in our oceans. The poor sharks get a bad rap. They are some of the most misunderstood animals on the planet, and no one but divers like me and marine biologists try to set the record straight and speak for the shark, which doesn't have the right of the free press or its own advertising agency to defend itself.

Let me share a story with you to explain my point. I remember reading a story in a newspaper and hearing it repeated many times on TV news as another worldwide headline. Many years ago, a shark killed a young boy in the waters off a Florida beach. It was a sad story. Anytime a child is attacked by any animal, it is brutal, but sometimes we need to look deeper into the story. If it wasn't bad enough already, the news dwelt on the killing of a child and made everyone think negatively about sharks, even to the point of making people wonder why sharks even exist in our waters. Later, I researched the story; here is what really happened, which we never read in that article.

A father and son were fishing off the coast one night, and the boy had a stringer of fish, which they had previously caught, hanging on his belt in the water. Both were fishing in waist-deep water at the time, when suddenly a bull shark attacked the boy. Bull sharks are notorious beach feeders and are the most likely shark to bite a beachgoer, since they usually prefer shallow water to hang out in. You will find them in abundance under the bridges along the Overseas Highway, one of the longest overwater roads in the world. It runs from the mainland to Key West, connecting some forty-two bridges.

So here was the inside story. Here was a father and son fishing in waist-deep water; the boy had bloody fish hanging on his fishing creel near his leg when the shark attacked. The father should have known better than to allow his son to have bleeding fish in the water, especially on his young son's leg. The shark smelled the blood, came in, and grabbed the fish and the boy's leg all at the same time; the boy unfortunately bled to death from the attack.

You cannot blame the shark. After all, it was coming in for a free meal with no intentions of killing anyone. But the news never reported that part of the story; instead, it appeared to blame the shark once again, and we wonder why people are afraid of sharks. This type of story plays out over and over all over the world. The same things happen to surfers; a shark attacks someone, thinking it is a seal, but it is mistaken identity for the most part.

There are over four hundred distinct species of sharks, and they vary in size, diet, and habitat; but the vast majority are harmless to humans. In fact, two-thirds of all shark attacks involve only three species of sharks: the great white, the tiger shark, and the bull shark. Bull sharks tend to take more human lives each year than the others, simply because they are closer to beaches. The tiger shark is the most vicious, based on reports I have heard. Both tigers and great whites prefer deep waters and seldom come in to shallow waters.

Let me illustrate their aggressive tendencies. Pretend you were swimming in the ocean, all alone at sea, in shark-infested waters. It is helpful to understand the difference between a great white and a tiger shark's disposition. The great white and tiger shark differ greatly in their reactions to a human being in their habitat. The great whites, due to an absence of hands like all other sharks, tend to bump you in the water with their snouts to get a feel for what you are. They might take a bite, even take off your arm or leg, but then they would normally swim away, allowing you to die before coming back for you, giving you time to possibly escape before being attacked again. Tiger sharks, on the other hand, won't do that; they will strike and take their victim all at once.

I saw a film once about the tiger shark. On camera, two skin divers, who were out at sea, saw a tiger shark they believed to be a fourteen-foot female just off their boat. They wanted to take some pictures of her and to test whether they were safe to swim with her in the open ocean. They both got into the water, only too soon to be chased out of the water and back on the boat. They decided to let her settle down a bit; then, being braver than me, they got back in the water and dived deep down to try to find her. Find her, they did; she was on the bottom and had bitten another shark in half; it was half her size. She had already consumed the first half and was starting on the second half when they spotted her. She was aggressive and hungry, and the guys were lucky she hadn't attacked them earlier.

Recently, I read about a woman swimming in the ocean in cold waters off the coast of Maine in the very first shark attack ever recorded in that state's history. She was swimming in a seal area, about twenty yards off an island, while wearing a dark wet suit to protect her from the cold water. One of the problems is that people tend to imitate seals by what they wear. In many cold-water areas, surfers and swimmers put on a wet suit—most of which are black or gray, made to absorb sunlight and heat. Then they swim in areas where seals (the food of sharks) exist, setting themselves up as bait. You might as well put on a complete seal suit, because you appear as one, floating on the surface to a passing shark out there, searching for food. You might be killed by a shark attack but are seldom entirely eaten. A shark will take a bite but then leave you once it finds out you aren't a seal.

I tell you these stories not to scare you but rather to educate you. Yes, sharks kill people; I would never deny that. But I am here to help you understand that we humans aren't their intended food source. Humans have too bony of a structure. Sharks need fat in their diets; that is why they like seals. They don't search out humans to consume daily. But yes, attacks can and do occasionally happen, but think of this. Out of seven and one-half billion people on the planet, there are only about seven to ten shark attacks a year in the entire world. How big is that number? You have a better chance of being struck by lightning. In fact, shark attacks on humans are way down on the list when compared to most other animals. Do you know the critter that kills more humans than any other? Here is a hint; it is very small. Have you guessed it yet? It is known as the mosquito, with malaria topping the chart for the most human deaths.

Of the one hundred million sharks taken each year around the world, most are taken for only their fins. For example, the shark-fin soup in Asia serves as an aphrodisiac, which sells for over a hundred dollars a bowl—one of the most expensive seafood products served at weddings and special events. Even though most countries have banned shark finning today and now have even gone so far as to protect some sharks, foreign, pirate fishermen are still fishing for sharks just for their fins. They haul up a beautiful shark, cut off its fins, and throw them up on the ship's deck in stacks, then dispose of the live carcass, minus its fins, where it sinks to an agonizing death. It is cruel treatment; still alive, the shark sinks to the bottom, bleeding and unable to swim. It is later eaten by other sharks and other critters. It would be one thing if fishermen kept the entire shark for food, but they don't. They make room only for the fins aboard their ships. It is the same illegal mentality as taking the tusks off elephants for their ivory and leaving the rest of the animal to rot as we used to hear about years ago in Africa.

Illegal fishermen are paid hundreds and sometimes thousands of dollars for each fin alone. Because there is a market for shark fins, the finning will continue. They get more for the fins than for the entire shark, so they don't want the body of the shark, since it takes up too much room on deck; they want only the more expensive fins, which take up little space. This practice, known as "shark finning," uses only between one and five percent of the shark. Furthermore, without the bodies of the sharks, it is nearly impossible for fisheries managers and scientists to accurately identify and determine the exact number of sharks that are being killed.

As I promised earlier, let me give you some examples of how sharks work to help the ecosystem throughout the world. This is information I have earnestly and eagerly learned from the many marine biologists with whom I have met and visited for many hours while on liveaboard dive boats around the world. I have found that they have vast, rich information I am willing to share.

Scientists estimate that fishing has reduced large predatory fish populations worldwide by ninety percent over the past fifty to one hundred years. Thereby, sharks represent the largest group of threatened marine species on the

International Union for Conservation of Nature's (IUCN) red list of threatened species. Yet only three of the four-hundred-plus shark species (basking sharks, whale sharks, and great white sharks) are protected to date from the pressures of international trade. The remaining species are ignored or seen as low priority despite their important role in their ecosystems. Another factor is the slow rate of reproduction of the sharks, with these incredible numbers of sharks being taken; what most people don't understand is that it takes twelve to twenty years for some sharks to even begin to reproduce. So their reproduction rate is a very slow process, even if we stopped killing all sharks today, which isn't happening.

No wonder we don't see many sharks while diving anymore. I remember going into schools, colleges, and universities and giving talks. The students' first question, when I told them I swam with and filmed sharks, was, "Are you not afraid of being attacked by a shark?" Again, there's the *Jaws* image at work. When I tell them that people are instead the real culprit—killing as many sharks as we do—they end up better understanding and becoming friends of the shark; and by my educating them, they realize and are also upset to learn that humans kill so many.

I have always enjoyed talking to young people in schools and at churches about the underwater marine life. In fact, I even became a speaker for the Oceans for Youth Foundation at one time, going into high schools and elementary schools and showing clips furnished by the foundation to teach kids about the environment of our oceans and the abundant sea life. Oceans for Youth, a nonprofit organization, was started by the famous Jacques Cousteau family.

Talking to a class in a school gym at Bear Lake, Michigan

As top predators, sharks are worth their weight in gold by doing the work they do, and man doesn't give them any credit at all as they help to manage healthy ocean ecosystems. In fact, speaking of gold, sharks also influence the economy through ecotourism. In the Bahamas, for example, a single live reef shark is worth upward of two hundred fifty thousand dollars due to dive tourism versus a one-time value of fifty dollars when caught by a fisherman. One whale shark in Belize can bring in as much as two million dollars over its lifetime.

As the number of large sharks decline, the oceans will suffer unpredictable and devastating consequences. Sharks help maintain the health of ocean ecosystems, including sea grass beds and coral reefs. Healthy oceans depend on sharks. But now that I have painted somewhat of a clear picture of the shark decline, let me give you a few examples of its rippling effect in our ecosystem, which you aren't being told about.

Surveys show that the abundance of the eleven great shark species (sharks more than two meters in length) along the eastern coast of the United States has declined to levels of functional elimination. This means that sharks are now unable to perform their ecological role as top predators. All the species in this area, except for the mako shark, have declined by more than 50 percent in the past eight to fifteen years. Scalloped hammerhead, white, and the thresher shark abundances are estimated to have declined by more than seventy-five percent in the past fifteen years. During this same period, their prey—twelve species of rays, skates, and smaller sharks—have increased in abundance by as much as tenfold.

The effects of this decline have cascaded throughout the entire ecosystem, resulting in the collapse of the century-old scallop fishery. The species that increased most in abundance was the cownose ray, which migrates up and down the eastern coast, consuming scallops, clams, and oysters. By 2004, bivalve predation by cownose rays had removed most of the bay scallops, terminating the North Carolina fishery. Without bay scallops to eat, the cownose rays—along with other rays, skates, and small sharks— are expected to expand their foraging to clams and oysters. This is already being seen in the loss of another bivalve, a hard clam known as the "quahog." The decline of the quahog, a key ingredient in clam chowder, is forcing many restaurants to remove the American classic from their menus.

The further disappearance of scallops and clams demonstrates that the elimination of sharks can cause irreparable harm to the economy in addition to the ecosystem. Shifts in species abundance aren't the only consequence of removing top predators, since habitats can also be altered. Hungry rays roaming the waters and hunting for food have the potential of uprooting seagrass at higher rates, leading to poorer-quality nursery grounds for fish. Additionally, bivalves are not only a food source for rays but also a filtration system for the ocean. Bivalves feed on phytoplankton flat, which they filter from the water column. This helps to maintain a high level of water quality. With the decline of scallops, clams, and other bivalves, this filtration system is disappearing. As a result, already-stressed coastal areas could experience additional uncontrolled algae blooms and dead zones, again damaging ocean ecosystems. Just like a swimming pool with a broken filter, a coastal environment without bivalves could choke the blooms of uncontrolled algae. This is an example of what the loss of sharks is doing to the fishing industry.

In review, what this simply means is that with the lack of sharks patrolling the reefs, when they were once in abundance, the cownose rays and southern stingrays have now taken over and consume the shell fish, scallops, oysters, clams, and other shell fish all valuable to the fisheries industry. So, with the sharks gone, the other marine life mischievously play. But when sharks are patrolling, the other marine species seem to stay out of mischief.

Next, let me give you an example of what the lack of sharks is doing to the coral reef systems. Healthy coral reefs provide a complex, three-dimensional habitat that promotes species diversity and abundance. The loss of sharks in a reef ecosystem, like that of the Caribbean Sea, can trigger a chain reaction felt throughout the entire food web, ultimately leading to the degradation of coral reefs on a local and even regional scale. Since macroalgae compete with coral for settlement on reefs, coral depend on herbivorous fish, otherwise known as vegetable-eating fish, to graze the algae and provide space for coral to settle and grow. A reduction in herbivorous fish prevents coral from thriving. The loss of sharks as top predators in the ecosystem allows the number of grouper and other carnivore fish to thrive. The groupers in turn reduce the number of herbivores, such as parrot fish, blennies, and gobies in the ocean. Without these herbivores to eat the algae off the coral, algae will take over a reef system. This overgrowth of macroalgae makes the habitat homogeneous, minimizes the number of available niches for fish species, and decreases the species diversity.

Again, the shifts in the abundance following coral decline change the overall species diversity and composition of the entire reef system, which even affect fish species; these rely on the live coral. The removal of sharks from the coral reef ecosystem can ultimately affect the resilience of coral reefs to disturbance, leading to declines in species diversity and abundance.

The coral reefs in Jamaica, for example, demonstrate this shift from a healthy state to a damaged one. Over the past thirty to forty years, the species composition in Jamaica has changed drastically. Sharks, snappers, jacks, triggerfish, and groupers are now replaced by small, herbivorous fish. Along with this change in species composition, coral abundance has declined from more than fifty percent in the late '70s to less than five percent in the late '90s. Even though the remaining small fish are herbivores, they are too small (more than half are below reproductive size) to reverse the shift from a coral- to algae-dominated system. Because coral cannot compete, macroalgae now cover more that ninety percent of the reefs. Jamaica provides a clear example of the time and scale on which a shift from coral to algae can occur due to the loss of sharks from an ecosystem.

Simply put so you can understand this better, without sharks to patrol the reefs, the carnivores take over, just as when the police are away. the devils play. The carnivores, being meat-eating fish, eat the herbivores, the vegetable-eating fish. Therefore, there are no longer any herbivores to clean the algae off the reefs, and the reefs die from not being cleaned. End of story.

After diving around the world, I have seen this same scenario play out on reef systems all over—all due to the lack of sharks—from Australia, where much of the Great Barrier Reef is now dead, to many of the exotic islands. Why? Because man has again upset God's overall ecosystem plan for the once-rich oceans.

A third example concerns sleeper sharks in Prince William sound in Alaska. Models of spatial and dietary shifts of harbor seals in response to sleeper sharks provide another example of shark intimidation, resulting in behavioral modifications of prey species and a change in the abundance of commercially important fish species. Even though mortality from sharks is low, harbor seals alter their habitat and foraging in response to predation pressure. The two top prey items for seals in this area are Pacific herring and walleye pollock. Herring are fatty fish that congregate near the surface of the water and are often widely dispersed. Pollock, on the other hand, are found in deeper, colder water. Pollock caught by the fisheries industry are used predominately as a preferred fish for the making of fish sticks in our country. Though also preferred by sharks, pollock are larger and have more continuous distribution, which makes them a more predictable resource for seals.

When sleeper sharks are present, shark intimidation reduces seal foraging in the deeper waters and therefore directly increases the mortality of herring while decreasing the mortality of pollock. The health of the seal dictates how much risk it is to assume. For example, if herring is scarce and the seal's energy state is poor, it is more willing to venture into deeper water in search of the pollock. The removal of sharks changed this response by releasing seals from fear, allowing them to increase their use of the deep waters to consume pollock and decrease their foraging of herring at the surface. The presence of sleeper sharks directly alters the behavior of their prey. These changes can alter the population density and fitness of other species as well. Species at lower levels in the food chain may experience declines or even extinction from the disruptions resulting from chain reactions in the ecosystem. When the behavioral responses of prey species are altered, the changes in their foraging patterns can cause a cascading impact throughout the food web.

Do you still need more examples as to why sharks are important?

When one marine life dwindles to almost extinction, it has a rippling effect down the food chain that affects other marine mammals. Man harvests the pollock, the fish from the Alaskan waters, I talked about above; seals eat pollock and other small fish, anchovies, and so forth. If the supply is dwindling, as it is today from overfishing, the seals begin to die off from lack of food supply, and they decrease in numbers. When that happens, the sharks and killer whales have no food supply, since they normally feed on seals; so the sharks and killer whales turn to smaller marine life like sea otters, but unfortunately they have no fat content to keep these larger fish alive. So now the shortage of seals and other marine life, which feed on pollock, harvested by man, takes the sharks and killer whales out with them. As you can see, it is a never-ending cycle, and some species are already near extinction. All fish and marine life depend on one another to survive, just as God intended.

There are hundreds of examples of the ripple effect on our ocean's ecosystems due to the lack of sharks. I could fill up this entire book with examples, but I have many more things to tell you about. Sorry to go into so much detail, but I wanted to educate you about marine biologists' concerns; and as you can see, there are many.

One final note, though. Many people at my seminars and talks always ask me, "What can we do to help?" There are three key steps to protect sharks today. First, reduce the number of sharks captured in commercial fisheries through improved shark management, including requiring strict species-specific fishing quotas and stock assessments. Then truly end shark finning by requiring that all sharks be landed intact with their fins still naturally attached. And finally, reduce the demand for shark products such as shark-fin soup and other shark by-products.

Chapter 14

Great White Sharks

The great white sharks of Guadalupe Island, Mexico, would become show number eight.

I was excited to finally go on a once-in-a-lifetime dream shark dive and witness firsthand what a great white shark would look like up close and personal from a cage below the boat and be just feet away from one of the ocean's largest predators. I decided, since this was a special trip out, that I would interview all the boat's passengers along with this rather unique, small group of divers. I wanted them to tell me why they had decided to go down under and look at a great white eye to eye. I would get some very interesting answers and some funny ones as well, as you will see if you get a chance to see the show.

I, on the other hand, wanted to see firsthand what they looked like swimming near me in their own natural environment; I came away with a newfound admiration for this mightiest of sharks and an appreciation for how they live and move under the ocean. They had a girth much larger than one could put their arms around, not that you would ever want to do that. As much as I respect them, I am not stupid enough to get in the water in front of one without a cage. Funny thing, though—our captain and host of the trip told us first up that the cages weren't to keep sharks from attacking us but rather to keep divers inside, since there were always a few camera-unintimidated divers who would indeed venture outside the cage if left unattended. We were told this practice isn't allowed, to my sound agreement.

After all, these sharks weighed several tons, and on the first day out, we anchored in the deep waters offshore from the island. When they put the bait out, our first great white came into view. He came in so fast and hard that he ran into one of the two cages, knocking over the divers in the cage below and making a very loud bang topside, because it hit the cage with its full weight. Now how about it? Anyone ready to get suited up next to go down?

Shark cages hanging off the back of the boat at Isla de Guadalupe

Show 8: *The Great White Sharks of Guadalupe Island, Mexico* (Filmed in September 2006)

The box cover to our show says the following:

> Come with us aboard the luxury dive boat *Solmar V* as we leave the southern Baha Peninsula port of Ensenada, Mexico, en route to Isla de Guadalupe, Mexico. There we dive in cages with the largest and most feared sharks known to man, the apex predator, "the great white shark." This island is one of the greatest places in the world to see these gigantic sharks up close and personal and in the clearest possible waters, with up to one hundred fifty feet of visibility. These magnificent creatures average nine to fifteen feet in length and weigh around thirty-five hundred pounds. They are extremely graceful as they swim around in their natural habitat. Great whites can range in size of up to twenty-five feet long and weigh as much as seven thousand pounds or three and a half tons. They feed primarily on seals. On this special *Dive Travel* adventure, hear firsthand stories told by our divemaster and the boat crew, who work with these gigantic creatures of the sea daily. Then come with us on a topside tour of the island by boat. This island, formed by volcanic action with its rough and rocky shore, is complete with its own food source of harbor seals, elephant seals, and birds, which attract the great white sharks to this region. Now sit back and watch this exciting adventure into the deep, clear-blue waters of Isla de Guadalupe as we encounter our first great white shark.

The star, a great white shark

The reason Guadalupe, Mexico, is the best site to see great white sharks is simply its clear water, unlike the waters off Australia; Cape Town, South Africa; and the Farallon islands off California, where visibility is less than thirty feet. In Guadalupe, with one hundred fifty feet of visibility, we could see the great whites coming in from far off, unlike in thirty feet of visibility, where we couldn't see them until they were right upon us.

My first time in a cage was exciting, and when I viewed my first great white, I felt awe inspired, seeing him in his natural environment—knowing I was now in his living room, uninvited by him. As much as I had always liked sharks, I now had an even greater respect and appreciation for these giants of the deep and how they survive day to day. Later we got to take turns going down even deeper, one by one, in an open-topped cage, which was lowered and raised each time with a pulley system deep below the boat to see an overview of the cages above us and the sharks swimming overhead and sometimes even closer to us. Had a shark wanted to attack us, we would have been an easy target, being more out in the open.

Inside a cage and filming the great white sharks show

I always told my kids and grandkids that if I was ever harmed by a sea creature, they weren't to blame the critter, since I was the one in their living room; they weren't in mine. I was the invader; I was to be the one totally to blame, not them for defending their territory. But I always found that if you treat them with respect and not frighten or abuse them, they will do the same to you, just like most animals topside. Our dive course always taught us not to touch any marine life or coral, spreading oils and bacteria from our hands, and so forth, since it's not ours to touch, even though some still try it. It's like any other sport; there are always those who challenge and abuse the system and give diving a bad name by disobeying the rules.

Later in the week, we took a boat ride around Guadalupe Island and saw all the seals, both young and old, that lived on the rocky shore of the island. I felt sorry for them, wondering which ones were soon going to be the next victim of a great white shark attack just off the shore. It reminded me of why seals like to get out of shark-infested waters in other areas; after all, they aren't dumb. In other areas I used to see seals along the Santa Barbara, California, shoreline; they were resting and completely covering the tops of sailboats in the harbors off Santa Cruz—a hot spot and breeding area off California for great whites—or seals resting on top of buoys to stay out of the water in great white shark territory.

An Interesting story comes to mind. When I was in Santa Barbara, California, years prior, there was in the local newspaper an article about recent sightings of great white sharks on beaches off Santa Barbara. A person was directing his or her comments to the city fathers, accusing them of not warning tourists of sharks; the story sounded much like the city in the *Jaws* movie. One local surfer had even reported seeing one near him while surfing.

On our taxi ride back to the airport at the time, we asked the driver about the sharks, since he said he was a local surfer. I asked him about his thoughts of surfing with great whites in the area. His comment was that he hadn't ever heard anything about them. He was totally ignorant of the fact. All I remember thinking was, *He is a young guy, and young guys don't read newspapers.* He was just like the seals; he had no idea of what was out there, waiting for him. Surfers sometimes have been hit by attacking sharks; the reason for most of this is believed to be mistaken identity, with the surfer imitating a seal floating on the surface. The Interesting fact is that even those bitten by sharks always end up saying they don't blame the shark for the attack, even if they lost an arm or leg. They never seem to hold a grudge against the animal being in its own environment, and that is the correct response.

While great white sharks are big by today's standards and at the top of the food chain for marine animals, they are indeed no match for the orca, which holds the real top-of-the-food-chain title. The orca or killer whale is a toothed whale belonging to the oceanic dolphin family, of which it is the largest member. Orcas are some of the world's most powerful predators. They are immediately recognizable by their distinctive black-and-white coloring. Smart and social, orcas make a wide variety of communicative sounds, and each pod has distinctive noises its members will recognize even at a distance. They use echolocation to communicate and hunt, making sounds that travel underwater until they encounter objects, then bounce back, revealing their location, size, and shape. Though they often frequent cold, coastal waters, orcas can be found from the polar regions to the equator. They have very diverse diets, feasting on fish, penguins, and marine mammals, such as seals, sea lions, sharks, and even whales with teeth that can be up to four inches long. Orcas hunt in pods, with family groups of up to forty individuals.

I have witnessed them only while swimming near our dive boat once, and that was in the Bay Islands of Honduras. I have always enjoyed studying them, but they are the one creature I didn't have the opportunity to dive with or film up close, even after being in Alaska, where they are frequently found. Adult males can reach up to twenty-six feet in length and weigh up to twelve thousand pounds. Even as big as they are, they have never been known to attack a human out in the open ocean. So far that has happened only in captivity in marine parks.

Recently, however, there have been unusual attacks on boats and yachts by orcas or killer whales off the coast of Portugal and Spain. Some of the boats were severely damaged losing parts of their rudders and scaring deckhands on board. The attacks reportedly went on for up to forty-five minutes at a time, spinning the boats ninety degrees. Crews reported that the animals bit the rudder and started shaking it while the wheel was spinning from side to side. One of the British sailors who had sailed around the world said he had never seen orcas come that close before and said his boat had to be rescued after the attack. After docking, he realized how close the orcas had come to overturning the boat.

News of attacks so frightened Spain's Ministry of Transportation, they announced that sailing vessels forty-nine feet long or less were banned from sailing in the area where attacks had taken place. Most of the attacks were reportedly made by three large or juvenile killer whales. Scientists think they know why the boats were attacked. They seem to think the Killer whales might have suffered some sort of injury by boats and may have felt threatened. This is not the first time such attacks have happened throughout history though. Reports of Killer whales ramming boats go all the way back to the 1800s. However, killer whales are not the only marine life to ram a boat.

I am reminded of the legendary, historic event that took place on November 20, 1820 when the famous ship the *Essex*, an eighty-seven foot, two hundred and thirty-eight-ton American whaling ship set sail from Nantucket on a routine voyage to hunt whales for their oil. This whaling ship was rammed not once but twice by an injured giant, eighty-five-foot-long bull sperm whale. The ship later sank at sea after being destroyed.

This was one of the greatest true stories ever told in several chilling books about the *Essex*. It later went on to inspire another novel in the tale of *Moby-Dick*. What man did to our whales—killing thousands almost to near extinction during those early years, savagely mutilating them in our oceans around the world for simply obtaining riches from their blubber when boiled into oil—was very disturbing. It has been estimated that more than two hundred and twenty-five thousand sperm whales were harvested around the world during the 1800s. This may have reduced the entire sperm whale population by as much as seventy-five percent. Only the blubber was obtained from these giant whales, while the rest of their bloody massive carcasses was left to float and rot at sea.

This slaughter is like what happened to the elephants across Africa when only their ivory was taken due to the greed of hunters. I have always found myself rooting for these magnificent, defenseless behemoths that God created. I recognize that some intelligent marine animals finally stood up to man's greedy actions, fighting back to retaliate and defend themselves against invading boats and ships at sea. Sperm whales, thankfully, have now recovered and are once again roaming our oceans.

Holding my camera on a liveaboard dive boat off Guadalupe Island, Mexico

Chapter 15

Diving in Costa Rica, Turks, and Caicos Islands

Our local dive shop was in the process of setting up two more trips to go diving: the first one to Costa Rica and the second to the Caribbean Islands of Turks and Caicos. These were two more trips I could film for future shows now that I had been catching up on the previous shows in the series.

Show 9: *Costa Rica on the Pacific Side of the Country* (Filmed in February 2000)

On this *Dive Travel* adventure, we fly into the city of Liberia in Costa Rica and stay at the beautiful Ocotal Beach Resort, located on a high bluff overlooking a scenic bay on the Pacific Ocean coast. We arrive during "green season," when the waters of the Pacific are tinted green. Visibility is only about thirty feet, but what these waters lack in visibility they make up for in an abundance of aquatic marine life. *National Geographic* calls Costa Rica "one of the most biologically intense places on earth." It is here that we will encounter our first whale shark, see a cloud of hundreds of cownose rays swim over our heads, and see countless schools of Pacific fish. We will dive some of the most popular dive locations Costa Rica has to offer, including the famous Bat Island, known for bull sharks, as well as Catalina, Buda, Palmares, Virador, Fatboy, Black Rock, and Widow Reefs. The high-cliff shoreline and jagged rocks pointing up out of the ocean floor at various dive locations are breathtaking and yet somewhat eerie, peaking up out of the waves from the sea. We will visit a local Costa Rican triathlon in action to get a sense of local flavor. On this trip, we also take a road venture cross country to Mount Arenal, South America's largest active volcano, at an elevation of five thousand four hundred thirty-six feet. The volcano, dormant for four hundred years, came alive on July 29, 1968, and has been active, spewing hot, molten lava ever since. At night you can see fire and lava flowing down the volcano's side of the mountain. So sit back and join us in exploring the beautiful Pacific Coast of Costa Rica.

We found the diving interesting despite the lower-visibility "green-water" period. At other times of the year, the green water doesn't exist, and it is clearer. The abundance of cownose rays was incredible as they swam in clouds above and around us.

One day while diving under the ocean, several divers headed out in front of us. Suddenly, they came rushing back toward us just as a small whale shark came over the reef and turned right in front of my camera. I was excited, since this was my first sighting of a whale shark. He was small, but having said that, he was still larger than any fish I had seen to date, at least fifteen feet long and very big around.

Whale sharks, the largest fish in the ocean, aren't whales but rather sharks, though they have a lot in common with whales. They are massive like whales, and they feed more like whales than a typical shark. Whale sharks can get up to forty feet in length or about the size of a school bus, but on average they are about eighteen to thirty-two feet and weigh twenty tons or as much as forty-seven thousand pounds. This slow-moving shark holds many records for sheer size in the animal kingdom, most notably being, by far, the largest living, non-mammalian vertebrate. Whale sharks are now protected and can live up to seventy years or more in the wild. They are found in many areas of the world, sometimes swimming in groups. They have flattened heads with blunt snouts above their mouths. A whale shark's mouth is about five feet wide. They have rows of over three hundred teeth, but as filter feeders, they don't use these teeth to eat. Plankton is their main source of food, but they can also eat shrimp and small schools of fish, algae, and other marine plant material, including sardines, anchovies, mackerels, squid, tuna, albacore, and fish eggs. They open their mouths to let water and the food come in, while their bodies filter out the food and release the water and any debris back into the ocean. They are gentle creatures of the sea and not as dangerous to humans as sharks can be.

The road trip to see the countryside in Costa Rica was awesome along with the trip to Mount Arenal, where we saw red-hot lava streaming down the sides of the mountain in the darkness of night, cutting a path and burning through trees as it found its way down the side of the volcano. The night always drew a small crowd of watchers. Little did I know that I would soon be back in that country a second time, only this time to visit the capital city.

Following our trip to Costa Rica, we changed planes in Miami and flew on to the Turks and Caicos Islands in the Caribbean.

Show 10: *The Turks and Caicos Islands* (Filmed in February 2007)

> One look at the geography of the Turks and Caicos Islands, and it's no wonder this place is called wall-diving central, with depths just offshore approaching twelve thousand feet. The Turks and Caicos are about an hour-and-a-half flight from Miami, Florida, and are made up of two chains of islands totaling twelve islands in all. Perched atop a shallow bank, separated by a trench-like channel, the twelve islands include West Caicos, Providenciales, North Caicos, Middle Caicos, East Caicos, South Caicos, Long Cay, French Cay, Grand Turk, Gibbs Cay, Cotton Cay, and Salt Cay. The three main islands—Providenciales, (aka Provo), Grand Turk, and Salt Cay—all sit front and center on deep ocean passages lined with vibrant coral reefs. Dropping over the edge of these vertical, steep walls creates a pulse-pounding rush! Provo is the most developed. It is a cosmopolitan island with an abundance of big resorts, restaurants, casinos, and clubs. It is a great getaway, with some of the longest, white-sand beaches in the Caribbean. The island also offers many non-diving options, from parasailing over gorgeous Grace Bay to taking windsurfing lessons. Meanwhile, on quirky and quiet Grand Turk, donkeys and roosters have the right-of-way, and the locals gather each evening to make music. Join us on this *Dive Travel* adventure as we dive the beautiful reefs and the crystal-clear waters below with the crew of *Caicos Adventures* dive boats, located on the main island of Provo.

After making a few dives right way, we found the waters were crystal clear and much like what we had seen in Cozumel, Mexico. The towns hadn't been developed too much yet and were laid back for anyone expecting to see a more vibrant city.

Just two months later, in April 2007, I was invited on what I thought was a trip of a lifetime! It ended up being wonderful indeed, but it was also the longest jet ride across the world I had ever been on "down under." I had met a dive buddy at one of my shows I attended and was invited to be taken around southwest and northwest Australia in what would be booked as a month-long tour. So here I go again for show number eleven.

Chapter 16

Let Us Go Down Under

Show 11: *Southwest Australia, a Diving and Sailing Adventure* **(Filmed in April 2007)**

The DVD box cover for the show says:

> Travel with us to the opposite side of the world from the United States down under for this exciting
> sailing and diving adventure into beautiful southwest Australia, home to koalas, emus, and kangaroos.
> I arrive in Perth, the west-coast capital, and travel south down the coast, diving along the way from
> Perth to Busselton, in this first of a two-part series. Join us as we board the seventy-foot *Tarquin*, a
> Ferro/cement sailing vessel, and sail down part of the coastline. Included in our visit are the cities of
> Perth, Rockingham, Fremantle, and Busselton, where we dive the Busselton Jetty, a dock extending
> a mile out into the ocean, and tour the *Swan* shipwreck offshore. The jetty is one of the longest docks
> in the world. We also visit Rottnest Island, home of the quokkas. In the seventeenth century, Dutch
> explorers could well have been horrified to find these giant rats on the island. They call it Rottnest,
> meaning "rat's nest," a very unflattering name for a place that is now the nearest holiday/vacation
> island to Perth. The quokkas, which resemble cute, tiny miniature kangaroos more than rats, are now
> protected, and It is the only place in the world where they are found. We also dive and take a tour
> of Seal Island, where we find beautiful swim-through arches and see some soft coral and vegetation
> below the ocean along with the unique fish of the region. View the countryside and enjoy southwest
> Australia from down under on this special edition of *Dive Travel*.

It was decided that I would come to Perth in Southwest Australia to begin filming. Since the Great Barrier Reef,
the largest reef system in the world on the east side of Australia, was mostly dead or dying, my host invited me
instead to film the Ningaloo reef, Australia's longest, fringing reef system. It is considered the most pristine reef on
the island. However, located in the east, it is on the opposite side of the country from where the Great Barrier Reef
is located, on the west coast. This means I would fly into Brisbane, in east Australia, first, where Quanta airline
would land from the USA; I would then need to travel across Australia four more hours to the west side. It was
much like the USA in size, so it would be like traveling from New York City to Los Angeles, a four-hour flight,
adding to my already twenty-six hours of flying time just getting to Australia from the USA. Australia, unlike
the USA though, is backward in that the north side of Australia is hot like the USA's southern side, and southwest
Australia is very cold like our north. When I arrived, my friend, David, had a large sailboat, which we called home
for the first two weeks of the trip as we traveled in the southwest part of Australia.

What I wasn't aware of exactly was how cold the water was in the south. I had brought along a three-mill suit;
mill means the thickness of the fabric. I ended up having to purchase a new five-mill suit from a dive shop before

I could complete the dives there; the water was *that* cold. I found the temperature there surprising. Since I was traveling southward from the USA, I was expecting it to be warmer. I failed to account for its being so far removed from the equator where it is always warmest.

While I enjoyed diving around Seal Island at the time I filmed it, it would be years later when I would learn that the island was a great hangout for great white sharks. Had I known that I might not have spent my day filming there, mostly alone. But back then, apparently no one had known of any sharks being sighted there. I found sailing on the sailboat fascinating; this was my first time on a quite large sailboat for diving. This one was a beauty, and the crew was second to none. The vessel skimmed along at a fast pace and was so quiet that all we could hear was the wind and the water as we slashed through the waves. I could hardly believe the boat was made of cement.

One day I walked out on the front of the vessel to get a bird's-eye view back over the ship. It was like walking out on a gang plank. But what a view I got of the sailboat with its high mast and the surrounding sea. If you get a chance to see the show, the video is great; you get to see the boat sail full speed ahead.

One day we visited a kangaroo park filled with baby kangaroos. They were all over me as I fed them before the camera. They are so cute, but the koalas won over my heart for cuteness, although they had very long toenails and could scratch me if I wasn't careful. We also visited the local emu, a tall bird like the ostrich. Emus are tall, flightless birds native to Australia. We opened the show in front of the landmark pavilion in Perth.

I found the cost of living a lot more expensive there than back in the States. Milk easily sold for five dollars per gallon. All food items, such as peanut butter, meats, cheeses, and cereal were about three times the price for American-made brands, but in the end it all seemed to even out, since wages for most Australians were three times that of normal wages in the USA. So both economies ended up being about the same.

Show 12: *Northwest Australia* (Filmed in April 2007)

> In our second of a two-part series from Western Australia, we continue to travel a northern route up the western coast along the Indian Ocean. The temperature begins to heat up the farther north we travel. The coral coast is in the hot and arid tropics of Northwest Australia. In Geraldton, we join up with the Batavia Coast Dive Academy and board Australia's only amphibious rescue helicopter to fly thirty-five nautical miles offshore to the famous Abrolhos Islands and dive their spectacular coral gardens, which offer a home to a unique mix of tropical and temperate marine species. With warm southern-flowing currents, it creates a marine environment that breeds both tropical and temperate sea life to thrive in an area where it wouldn't normally be found. Farther northwest, we visit Coral Bay, part of the famous Ningaloo Reef, heralded as the most pristine reef system in Australia. The Ningaloo Marine Park begins at about one hundred kilometers north of Perth. Our northwest last diving adventure culminates at Exmouth, a town built by the US Navy in the 1950s; it is home of the famous Navy Pier. Here a mass spawning of more than two hundred species of coral occurs in March and April each year and is part of a chain of biological events that herald the arrival of whale sharks. At Exmouth, we also dive around the famous Muiron Islands, a marine management park area. Sit back and watch the adventure unfold as we travel by camper through the bush country of beautiful Northwest Australia.

On our route, we passed many giant anthills made up of red sand from the soil; they stood many feet tall. One day we went out in search of whale sharks, as promised by the excursion. One thing I learned is that no one can guarantee success of seeing marine life. Although this boat offered a guarantee, if it didn't happen, they give you a trip out later to spot them. Unfortunately, I was only there one day, so we didn't get to see any. The coral bloom was rich along the shoreline, which was colored red. It had a somewhat sweet yet nauseating smell, which permeated the surrounding area. Whale sharks feed on this when the color bloom is in season.

I really enjoyed my time in Australia, but time went quickly. The coral reefs were colorful, and the water was clear and warm in the north, but the marine life was very similar to other species I had seen before in the Pacific. The three exceptions were the platypus, a strange-looking creature with a duck bill for a snout; the dugong, similar to what we call the Florida manatees; and the coral reef snakes. They had many smaller critters native to Australia as well.

On the helicopter ride to the island we had visited and back again, I obtained a lot of aerial footage over the coastline of the small islands and mainland. This was a very large cargo helicopter, larger than any I had flown in before; it was capable of holding many crew members. In fact, the captain had allowed me to be strapped into a harness assembly prior to lifting off, which gave me a bird's-eye view as I sat in the harness in the open doorway of the cargo craft, videoing the beautiful islands and sea below as we flew back from the dive trip. It turned out to be a real adrenaline rush for sure, with nothing holding me from falling out of the copter but the harness assembly. I had been in lots of helicopters and would be in many more to come, but never had I been strapped in a harness before quite like this one. *It was safe,* or so I thought, but still exciting.

Here's an interesting side note to this story: A short time after arriving back home, I received a request for my Australia DVDs to be sent to a state courthouse in Australia. It seemed the captain of the helicopter, whom I had interviewed on camera, hadn't supposed to have been flying the copter that day. It was Australia's only cargo rescue helicopter at the time, and it was supposed to be grounded for repairs. Wow! I thought about that with my partially hanging out of the doorway. Talk about high adventure! I was glad God was watching over our dive group that day. The court wanted proof that he had been flying. I felt bad for the captain since he had been super nice to us, but it was a court-ordered subpoena for my shows to be shipped immediately. A check was attached. When I heard later from him, he was upset but only with himself, and he was back to work.

The caravan ride across the terrain was the prettiest part of the trip; I saw wide-open, desert-like countryside with giant, red-colored anthills along the way. In other areas we saw scrub brush like out west, then on to rolling hills and valleys with lots of unexpected farm windmills in the foreground and off in the distant skyline. We stayed at some campgrounds along the way back, seeing some wild emus run through the park in the early-morning hours. It was pretty at sunset, especially with the kangaroos jumping around in the wild. It was certainly a beautiful country to visit. The air was arid and dry, much like Arizona.

Most of the people in Australia all live on the coastline around the island; only a few native tribes live in the center of the island, which is mostly vacant, undeveloped land. Flying from the east coast of Australia back to the United States and leaving Brisbane, I couldn't help but remember the Australian zoo located north of there and the country's icon Steve Irwin, the crocodile hunter who lived there. I had always enjoyed watching his many shows. Unexpectedly, in the next show I would find myself doing a tribute to him.

I loved the Australian culture and the accents of the people down under; listening to them talk was gentle and soothing to the ear. I really liked the western-flavored Australian folk music, songs like "Waltzing Matilda," "Tie Me Kangaroo Down Sport," and "True Blue," to name a few—all by different artists offering beautiful native sounds. I brought back a lot of the music to be used in the Australian series. I wanted to give viewers a taste not only of the video from a foreign country but also of the sounds from native exotic islands to make them feel like they were right there in person as I was.

The one thing I didn't care for was their famous Vegemite, which they put on toast; you hear about it in some Australian songs. Anyway, I apparently put too much of it on my morning toast one day to try, but I found it not only too burning and strong flavored but also unappealing for my taste buds. I was told to put on a thin layer next time, but I made sure there wasn't a next time. No worries, mate! It was a fun time, but soon I would be saying farewell to the song "True Blue," and I was off on that very long flight back home.

Picture of box cover for Northwest Australia showing helicopter

Chapter 17

Tribute to a Man and a Fish

Show 13: *The Famous Kelp Forest of California* **(Filmed in June 2007)**

The last show of 2007 was filmed in June off the coast of San Diego, California.

> On this dive adventure, we travel to sunny San Diego to dive the famous kelp forest in La Jolla Cove. The kelp forest stretches along the southern coast of California. La Jolla Cove is one of the few places in the San Diego area that features "clear," underwater visits year-round. It is the perfect place for snorkeling and viewing ocean life. Visibility is about thirty feet. The cove is protected from fishing and kelp harvesting; it is also maintained as a marine sanctuary. In unprotected areas, the kelp is harvested to make vitamins. We also dive with giant black sea bass, native only to that region in this cove. These giant sea bass range in size from sixty to three hundred pounds, with the largest growing up to five hundred pounds. While there, we offer a mini tribute both to a fish and to a man. We interview longtime native Rod Watkins, a NAUI instructor (National Association of Underwater Instructors) and owner of Scuba San Diego, my host. Rod tells us about a special marine friend of divers named "Blacky," a giant sea bass, about three hundred pounds in size. It would swim right up to greet divers and allow them to pet it with their gloves on. Unfortunately, a ruthless diver with a spear gun killed it, even though "Blacky" was in the protected waters of La Jolla Cove. Our tribute is also to a very special man, Steve Irwin, the famous crocodile hunter from Australia, who was loved the world over. Also in San Diego we encounter one of the area's largest concentrations of protected seals sleeping on the shoreline off the coast. As usual, *Dive Travel* takes you also on a city-wide tour of San Diego to show you some of the various attractions and the hospitality this Southern California city has to offer divers and visitors. We also tour the famous ship, the USS *Midway*, a naval aircraft carrier, harbored off the city's coast.

It was sad to hear Rod talk about "Blacky," the friendly sea bass. Divers were upset that he had been killed, for he had been a friend to many in the cove. But even more sad was the death of Steve Erwin. I had gone to Australia just a few months after his death and had learned some of the inside scoop as to why they think he got stung by the southern stingray.

They told me that Steve and his camera crew were filming in the reefs offshore during the season when tiger sharks tend to come in and around the reefs in search of stingrays for food. They think that at that time of year, the stingrays were more skittish than normal, and the fact that Steve and his cameraman were hovering over the stingray as a potential threat just added to the problem. The stingray was simply defending itself.

I, along with the entire world, was so in shock when this happened. We found it alarming that Steve's death was by a mere stingray, since stingrays don't normally exhibit this behavior. In fact, since keeping records, they said this was one of the first times on record a man has died from a stingray's barb. It is practically unheard of. My family and I used to watch many of Steve's shows of the "crocodile hunter" and really enjoyed them but always feared that someday he might get bitten by a venomous snake or succumb to a crocodile attack. Guessing it would be a stingray attack as a possible cause of death wasn't even on anyone's radar.

If that reality wasn't enough, the stingray shot its barb precisely into Steve's heart, causing so much pain, he immediately pulled it out, which resulted in his death. Had he left it in and been rushed to a hospital, he might have had a chance for survival, but by pulling the barb out, he ended up bleeding to death on location. You occasionally hear of stingrays shooting barbs into people's legs or arms, but hitting someone precisely in the heart, as if it were a target, was a first.

The kelp forest off San Diego was spectacular; we swam through it as if it were a jungle of sorts. It was there that I encountered a fish that just fell in love with my camera lens; he was such a ham! Seeing himself in the giant glass lens, which created a mirror reflection of himself, he must have thought he had found his true love at long last. I couldn't get rid of him, since every direction I turned, the fish followed. My dive buddy accompanying me on this dive was laughing the whole time.

Show 14: *Cocos Island* (Filmed in July 2007)

This show took me back again to Costa Rica. This time I flew into San José, Costa Rica, and began with a tour of the big city before boarding a dive ship for our long, four-hundred-mile boat destination to the island.

> Join us on this special diving adventure aboard the famous *Undersea Hunter* at Cocos Island (in Spanish: Isla del Coco). Cocos Island is a small, isolated island in the Pacific Ocean. The island, made from volcanic rock, rises to about twenty-eight hundred feet above sea level with a total area of nine square miles. Here, surrounded by deep waters with counter currents and rich nutrients, pelagic (open sea) animals of all sizes exist, from large schools of scalloped hammerhead sharks to a wide variety of marine life. The only residents permitted to live on the island are park rangers, located at two camps that patrol it as a no-fishing zone. For that reason, it is abundant with marine life, especially the elusive, giant, scalloped hammerhead sharks. Cocos Island receives on average six hundred inches of rainfall each year, which keeps its lush rain forest flourishing and alive with deep jungles and vegetation. It also feeds its many waterfalls both in and around the island. Rainbows appear over the island almost daily. It is believed that the most adventurous treasure in the world still lies on Cocos island. This treasure cache is estimated to be worth over $100 million. For that reason, Cocos Island is believed to be the real *Treasure Island* Robert Louis Stevenson wrote about. Legend has it that Michael Crichton visited the island and was so taken with its prehistoric-looking beauty that he was inspired to write *Jurassic Park*. He used the fictitious Isla Nublar, which is off the west coast of Costa Rica. Aerial shots of Cocos Island were used in the movie. Sit back and enjoy our tour of Cocos Island, truly one of the world's premier dive locations, on this edition of *Dive Travel*.

This was one of the most fun and informational dive shows I ever filmed. I fell in love with the island's cascading waterfalls, which were the first thing we noticed when our dive boat pulled up to anchor one early morning just before sunrise alongside the prehistoric-looking island. It truly looked like a scene right out of *Jurassic Park* all right. Big birds were flying up and out of prehistoric-looking rocks and caves. This island, owned by Costa Rica, is a national park, and no one is permitted on the island except its park rangers. However, one day the rangers allowed us to take an afternoon walk on the island and back through the jungles to a waterfall, which poured into a pool of water for swimming. That was an incredible adventure. To get there, we had to walk on a man-made hanging bridge made of used fishing lines and other fishing items rangers had confiscated from the ocean, along with boat lines left unclaimed by the violator fishermen.

The diving was incredible and is listed as one of the top destinations to dive, primarily due to the scalloped hammerhead sharks located offshore. The hammerheads are very timid when in a school such as this, since they are mating and don't like the bubbles coming off our scuba gear. In fact, the bubbles scare them so much that we had to hide behind rocks below the surface just to get any good pictures of the sharks. If these huge sharks saw a diver or saw or heard any air bubbles, they instantly darted off and didn't come close at all. Many times we tried to hold our breath to keep from expelling air bubbles, something we were trained never to do when diving, since we are always supposed to breathe naturally and never hold our breath when diving. But sometimes there are exceptions if you want to capture video or obtain a picture of them up close and personal.

As you can see, I had plenty of shots of them while I was there, especially near the end of our last dive, when I captured my famous scene used on the front of the box cover, with hundreds of hammerheads swimming overhead just as I was rising to the surface. I thank God for that. I think God really wanted me to get a parting shot of what He had created below the surface off beautiful Cocos Island. That day I got the best shot of all photographers on board. These great hammerheads are truly a gift from our almighty Creator.

School of scalloped hammerhead sharks off Cocos Island, Costa Rica

The two divemasters on board were a riot. They were so funny and entertaining. I had them do my dive tip of the week for this show; one of many dive tips is featured in each *Dive Travel* show. It is a tip of what divers should keep in mind for that dive destination. This time they prepared and offered the best dive tip of the week I ever filmed; then they added a second, which was so funny they had the boat crew in stitches. I ended up using both versions in the show. A good divemaster and host can make any trip fun and enjoyable if they just put a little effort into entertaining their guests, and this crew did all that.

After another successful trip to DEMA that year, I was invited to attend a dive shop, whose owner owned a rather large resort on Roatán, one of the three islands making up the Bay Islands of Honduras.

Chapter 18

Iguanas Galore

Show 15: *The Bay Islands of Honduras* (Filmed in February 2008)

Join us on this *Dive Travel* adventure series as we explore the western Caribbean Bay Islands forty miles off the northwest coast of Honduras. The three main inhabited islands include Roatán, Utila, and Guanaja—all part of the second largest coral reef in the world and one of Honduras' hottest attractions for scuba divers. Beneath the clear turquoise waters is a trove of unbelievable riches: vibrant coral, massive sponges, multicolored fish, and large pelagic (oceanic)species, like manta rays, sea turtles, and whale sharks. Surrounded by translucent waters painted in bold strokes of emerald greens and deep azure blue while surrounded by jungles of luxurious foliage and exotic flowers, these islands are a diver's paradise.

Roatán's history comes alive with tales of pirates. As many as five thousand pirates and buccaneers used the islands as a base for attacking Spanish galleons laden with precious metals, woods, and other New World bounty. Our first stop is on Roatán. Here at our host's Anthony's Key Resort, we examine their famed dolphin program, one of the world's best dolphin training centers. Four such centers exist on the planet. We also dive alongside reef tip sharks on a shark dive and explore the beautiful coral surrounding the island. We take you topside, tour the island, and visit a nearby iguana farm, home to three thousand iguanas. Then we are on to Utila, where we stay at the Deep Blue Resort, our host on that island, and dive the reefs and search for whale sharks. Utila is a backpacker's paradise—more rustic and remote. Original music from the CD *Welcome to Roatán* by Kristofer Goldman and the Culture Band is featured on this DVD (www.kristofergoldman.com). We hope you enjoy this DVD from the Bay Islands.

Well, the first time I lost my baggage was while traveling to this destination. It is always a chore making sure all my baggage is accounted for on and off planes to destinations; this was no exception. I usually carried three big, checked bags; a suitcase; my dive bag of dive gear; and my special underwater housing in a specially packed hard case, marked "fragile." Plus, I carried on my personal cameras in a bag and had a backpack. So there were five bags to cautiously watch over as I flew from destination to destination even in some third-world countries, where baggage is limited and can indeed get lost. But I have been blessed in my travels so far.

On this trip, the hard case with my housing arrived safely but no clothes or diving gear yet. I anxiously awaited their arrival, but they came three days later. Fortunately, I had my camera and housing so I could film, though none of my personal dive gear had arrived. But that didn't stop me from diving, since the dive shop loaned me their rental gear so I wouldn't miss any dives, which had been planned in advance for me. When the other two cases arrived three days later, I found out they had been sent on to another city. Out of all the shows I have made around the world, this was the only time I lost bags during travel. But in the end, I still got them delivered to me. Not bad for all my worldwide travels covering twelve years.

However, having said that, here is an example of an incident involving my underwater housing system in just one of my many travels:

The big, black, bulletproof, aluminum housing, with all its mystical wires and cords going both into and out of the housing that attached to the camera located inside, always looked suspicious to airport security. To be honest, it looked like a bomb in the making, especially since it included two rather large batteries that were later attached to those cables. After first purchasing the expensive system, I originally carried it with me inside a carry-on bag. The batteries had to be pre-packed separately though as checked-in luggage. But, even then, I always got used to being pulled aside after going through their high-tech scanning equipment when going through security. The apparatus was nearly always hand checked by staff to examine the merchandise on every flight I took.

Due to this always happening, I later bought a big, black, solid heavy-duty Pelican case that weighed close to seventy pounds when packed. This case had latches around it and a place for a lock.

The case, with its outside heavy-duty handles and inside foam compartments, carried it all—the housing, the camera, the underwater lighting system, batteries, and cables. I had put red stickers all around it that said, "Fragile, handle with care." Now, I could just simply drop off the heavy case at check-in with my suitcase and dive bag. I felt it was easier for them to check now, and I wouldn't have to answer questions at the passenger check in station.

For the most part, this always worked well. However, on one of my many Asian trips, I encountered an experience that would become my most intimidating experience ever. While waiting in the boarding lobby, we were all being called by name to board. I could not help but notice that everyone was leaving to board but me. When I was the only one left, I was approached by a military security guard and asked to follow him downstairs. Nervously, I soon found myself in a basement room with all cement walls that looked like a bomb shelter surrounding us. There, in the middle of the room, on the floor was my big, black case sitting all by itself. If it could have talked, I am sure it would be saying *"Please help me, master!"*

There were at least six or eight military men in uniform, all with military rifles standing around it in a circle, looking quite stern. I have to say, it was one of the only times I felt like a criminal. The guard asked me what was in it? He demanded I open it in front of them. Why they had not opened it before now, I didn't understand. I always had TSA locks on all the cases I carried that allowed security to check them. Apparently, the box looked too intimidating for them to open without me being present. Or maybe they just wanted me to be present to arrest if I had anything illegal in it. At any rate, I opened the box telling them I was an underwater videographer and film maker, and that the case simply carried my underwater equipment, which I showed them. The officers all looked on curiously, and finally, with a sigh of relief on my part, they were satisfied. I was escorted to the boarding area of the plane that was waiting to leave. I was met with puzzled looks on the faces of a full plane of passengers whom, I assume, were wondering why I was so late in boarding.

On another occasion, upon leaving a destination at customs, security tried to charge me a tax for my camera equipment. The officials assumed I had purchased all this equipment in their country and was transporting it back home. If carrying it all over the world was not enough of a burden, it seemed these extra episodes along the way just added to the frustration.

Meanwhile, the diving was great in the Bay Islands. We did a shark dive, in which we were surrounded by reef sharks, but they were all on their best behavior as they swam around us constantly, almost like being in a circus formation. They had placed some fish bait in containers on the ocean floor, which the sharks took turns cleaning up.

Later, I worked with some dolphin trainers at their training center for some education on how they trained the dolphins. This is one of four such training centers in the world; I ended up touring three of the four training centers, each in separate countries. There was one here, one in Grand Bahama Island, and one in Curaçao Island. Dolphins are special, smart creatures that can be easily trained, and it is amazing how dedicated they are to their trainers. They can take them out of their cages into the open ocean, and they don't try to escape but rather follow the boat back to their place of captivity since they know they are cared for and might not survive in the wild after being kept as trained dolphins. At night the dolphin trainers always put on a show for attending guests of the resort, to the delight of everyone.

One of the little-known treasures on Roatán is Sherman Arch's iguana farm. The farm is located along the main paved road in French Cay. The farm was started about eighteen years ago. Iguanas have long been the basic ingredient to make iguana stew in Roatán. To me, the stew didn't even sound very appetizing. While today the iguana is supposed to be protected, it is mainly protected only inside this farm. That is why they have so many who escape the hunters on the outside. The farm is a family operation with four children and a mother, who daily feed the critters. I cannot even imagine.

Upon arrival, I took a tour of the farm. They had tons of iguanas of all sizes—three thousand in all, to be exact—and they were right out in the open, and we walked through them in their front yard. They threw food to them, and they all raced to the food area as fast as their little feet would take them. The best time to arrive and see them was during feeding time. They even let us feed them if we wanted to. They can run fast. While I was videotaping them, they surrounded me. It was like, "Where shall I step next so as not to step on one of the critters?"

Lizards are somewhat intriguing to me but not one of my favorite animals on the planet. They all looked at me with their beady, little eyes, which seemed to penetrate me. They snuck up behind me while I had my back to them and was on my hands and knees to get some good closeup shots. I never knew just where they were at any given time. You can see in the show how big some were and how aggressive they were when they were feeding. It was an experience to see this many all in one setting. While it was interesting, I much preferred being back in the water.

One night I happened to hear Kristopher Goldman and his band, a local group, perform at the resort. I asked him if we could use his music for the show, which he agreed to. His songs were about the islands, and one song was about Roatán. His writing was great, and so was the band; they put on a great show for the guests at the dive club resort. When the show of the Bay Islands was completed, I sent him copies to sell over there for promotion in exchange for the use of his music. Almost all the music I used in my shows was original music reflecting the islands or countries I had visited, giving my audience a real feel of the island, matching it with my video.

After producing all my thirty-seven *Dive Travel* videos, I can hear all the music I used throughout the series. If you could hear them all at once, the music would literally cover the world, echoing music from every part of the planet. Each is unique in its own way, telling a story of diversity—humans praising God for the beauty the planet offers and the underwater scenes glorifying God's creations. I always receive a lot of compliments on the music I used in the shows. I guess I had developed a knack for that after being a disc jockey during the first sixteen years of my broadcast career. My expertise was production and blending sounds with scripts. I never would have been as apt in producing these shows today without my extensive broadcast career, which preceded my filming this dive series. Being in radio and television for a total of thirty-two years gave me a great background.

When I was over at the island of Utila, another one of the Bay Islands, we went out about every day on a boat, searching for whale sharks. Another diver and a doctor of marine biology were with me, and we had a few days to discuss whale sharks and how they were now being protected in most countries.

Unfortunately, we never came across any whale sharks off that island during our week-long time there. Again, you can never predict with any accuracy or guarantee to see them at any one time. So far, the only time I have come face-to-face with one under the water was in my dive show off Costa Rica. The doctor of marine biology told me they now count the whale sharks they encounter, and they are distinguished by the design and number of spots that appear on the topside of the whale sharks to identify them, much like a fingerprint is used on humans. The doctor was from Texas, and he invited me to come down sometime for some diving off the coast of Texas, but I never got around to making that happen.

Chapter 19

The Kiss of a Lifetime

In June 2008, I was invited to attend a dive seminar and tour off Grand Bahama Island. Thus, show number sixteen was filmed.

Show 16: *Grand Bahama Island* (Filmed in June 2008)

This time we travel to Grand Bahama Island, one of over seven hundred of the Bahama Islands in the Atlantic Ocean extending over five hundred miles, for a total of one hundred thousand square miles. Grand Bahama is called the second city, since it is the second largest city in the Bahamas and the second largest island in the chain. We take you under the ocean for a shark feed with reef sharks. The handlers have on full steel- mesh suits as they dish out the food to the awaiting, hungry sharks, while the sharks zoom over our heads. Later, we Join a dolphin training center, one of four such training centers in the world. This center takes dolphins out into the open ocean as they did in Roatán in the Bay Islands. But this time, the dolphins are taken out to greet snorkelers and divers in the open ocean. They could easily escape, but they don't. The *Dive Travel* host (me) gets the kiss of his life as shown on the box cover, right on his lips under the ocean by a large, five-hundred-pound female dolphin. Watch as the dolphins do tricks with divers and snorkelers both on the surface and below the ocean. These dolphins star in many Hollywood movies; we will show you one that is particularly a show-off as she poses for the photographers. As usual, we give you a topside view of Grand Bahama Island, its downtown, cruise ships, hotels, lighthouse, and the white, sandy, pristine beaches that extend for miles. Here we also attend a dive symposium and interview some of the key speakers and lecturers about diving these incredible, warm islands. You will see the reefs and the marine life, which make this such a special place in the Atlantic.

Trained Dolphin posing for cameras

While there, we did another planned shark dive, where the shark feeders wore steel, chained suits, while the rest of us sat around on the bottom of the perimeter of the shark feed, watching and photographing the session. It seemed like something was wrong here while we were sitting on the bottom, thinking about this scenario. Here they were in steel, chained suits, and we are just in our normal dive suits yet still pretty close to the critters; it perhaps appeared that we were a little underdressed for the occasion. I used to watch guys sometimes on the bottom when swimming over reefs; they used to take down a plastic water bottle and constantly squeeze it so it would make a crackling sound. They thought the sound would attract sharks, since it was akin to fish bones being crushed underwater, a sound that sometimes attracts sharks. I cannot say it ever really worked, but it sounded good.

Observing a shark feed off Grand Bahama Island

The dive crew had forewarned me that sometimes a handler, under the right conditions, may grab hold of a shark, flip it upside down, and put it in a trance. The shark handlers did just that. They picked up one of the sharks swimming by them, laid him on his back, and rubbed his belly; he was instantly in a trance. In the case of sharks, it has been observed in many different species, such as the lemon shark, reef shark, and tiger shark, that by simply placing them upside down, a state called "tonic immobility" is created. During this state, the shark's dorsal fin becomes straightened, and the breathing and muscle contractions become more relaxed. Many animals can enter a trancelike state, called "tonic immobility," whereby they appear dead in their surroundings. Some killer whales have learned to take advantage of this fact by using their tails to create currents in the water; the currents can turn a shark over so they can eat it. When they are upside down, their dorsal fins become straighter and more streamlined. Tonic immobility is also believed to be a breeding behavior in sharks, since rubbing them sometimes causes immobility. Simply put, by rubbing sharks in a specific position, one may put them in a type of sleep. After our shark handlers were finished subduing the shark, they turned it back over, and he swam away as if it were all a magic act. Here's a warning though: be sure not to try that on the next shark you see.

Finally, I attended my second dolphin training center on the island. I was assigned a trainer, and I learned a lot from her. First, they took me in the ocean, where I was to meet one of the star dolphins. Little did I know I was in for the kiss of my life. They instructed me before I got on the bottom of the ocean to take out my regulator breathing-apparatus mouthpiece so my lips were prepared for the dolphin to arrive for my soon-to-be "first kiss." Right on cue, as directed by her trainer underwater on the bottom of the ocean, she appeared in front of me and locked lips with me for what seemed like an eternity.

Yes, it was a very long time! I was wondering when I was going to get free to take a much-needed breath of air from my mouthpiece. Suddenly, just as she had approached me, she left me wanting more. My, what a fish she was, weighing in at over five hundred pounds. She really took my breath away. She seemed very large while kissing me, and she had a very powerful suction, too. All I could do was pucker up. The dive center took the picture, which appears on the cover of the Grand Bahama show, of this big dolphin kissing me. All in all, it was a pretty sweet experience.

What really amazed me was what happened the next day when I went over to the training facility. The trainer and I went out on a boat, accompanied by two of their specially trained dolphins. Both dolphins followed our small motorboat out into the ocean about a mile or more as they jumped and played behind us in the motorboat's waves and alongside the boat. I was amazed to have just witnessed them being captive inside their gated pens, but they were now swimming totally free in the open ocean, where they certainly could escape if they wanted to. But they stayed close to the boat as we kept going out farther and farther from shore.

Once we reached the destination to meet up with a snorkel boat from a cruise ship, we stopped, and the dolphins got ready to play, knowing they would be fed for each trick they performed. Two kids came off the boat, and they got to intimately play with dolphins for the first time in their lives. You could tell they were really excited and thrilled for this once-in-a-lifetime experience. The trainer instructed the kids on what to prepare for and then called the dolphins to action, and I filmed their antics and tricks with the kids for about a half hour.

During a lunch break, the trainer informed me, "You know, everyone thinks these dolphins are cute and cuddly," she said. "Well, the truth is, if they wanted to, they could take you out." I asked what she was referring to, and she said they had a woman once who had happened to poke a dolphin in the eye by mistake while petting it in the water, and the dolphin turned on her. She was bitten so badly that she had to be airlifted by helicopter to a hospital for treatment. I thought about that for a moment, thinking, *Well, the dolphin was only upset after being punched in the eye, so I guess I cannot blame him for his reaction to defend himself.* But it appeared the dolphins worked only for the fish treats given to them following all their tricks. The trainer said that yes, that was right; and that she was afraid to go into the open cages with them without treats.

Her words implied to me that perhaps some dolphins can be mean at times. I suppose they, too, have bad dispositions on some days. I asked her about what I had heard—that a pod of dolphins had saved a person at sea from sharks. She said that occasion was rare indeed. Instead, if a shark were to approach a dolphin, the dolphin would make a quick retreat. While the fish treats were fed to them, the dolphins were right on target with their mind-blowing talents of jumping and doing all sorts of tricks on demand.

Following the time with the kids, the dolphins used their fins to wave goodbye to the kids, and we were off, headed back to the training center as they leaped out of the water playfully all the way back alongside our boat and entered their cages like clockwork. They were happy to be back home, where they were fed and cared for. The trainer said the trained dolphins really didn't know how to catch live fish on their own in the open ocean and that it might be hard for them to survive on their own since they were now captive and being fed daily and taken care of. Or if they were attacked by a shark or another marine predator, they might not know how to respond or to defend themselves, not having had any such experience. So when they are taken out in the open ocean, they are eager to return home to their safe haven. I was just amazed by how they stayed close to the boat and never ventured off on their own. However, one training center told me that one dolphin did escape once. I always wondered how it cared for itself in the wild.

Box cover of Grand Bahama DVD showing dolphin kissing me

Chapter 20

Giant Megalodon Teeth

Show 17: *North Carolina Wreck Diving* (Filmed in June 2008)

On this *Dive Travel* adventure, join us as we stay in the USA and travel to Morehead City, North Carolina, to dive some of the shipwrecks that are part of the "Graveyard of the Atlantic." We interview Captain George Purifoy and his friend, Claude Hull, a history fanatic, about the *U-352* German submarine (sunk May 9, 1942). These men discovered the location of the sub (of which we give you a video tour) one hundred feet below the ocean's surface. Plus, we interview divemaster Bud Daniels and Claude Hull about the SS *Papoose,* a ship they also found. Other ships we tour on the ocean floor include the *SS Caribsea*, the USS *Indra*, the USCGC *Spar*, the USS *Schurz*, and the USS *Aeolus*. Most of these shipwrecks are surrounded and covered with marine life, including dozens of sand tiger sharks up to nine feet in length. We take you on a topside tour of the Morehead area and beaches, visit the new North Carolina Aquarium, which has a replica of the *U-352* sub surrounded by its own sharks; and we tour the city of Wilmington.

Sand tiger shark off Morehead City, North Carolina

In Wilmington, we search for the megalodon, prehistoric shark teeth. Megalodon sharks were the second largest predator on the planet, even larger than T rex., estimated to be forty to sixty feet long and weighing fifty-two tons. All total, megalodon had forty-six front-row teeth, twenty-four in the upper jaw and twenty-two in the lower. Most sharks have at least six rows of teeth, so a megalodon had about two hundred seventy-six giant five- to seven-inch-long teeth at any given time, capable of swallowing a hippopotamus whole. The teeth are found on a fossil ridge located forty miles out in the open ocean and under one hundred feet of water. I find two four- to five-inch teeth and many smaller ones. Those seven-inch teeth, when found, are worth upward of twenty thousand dollars and have become a treasure hunter's bonanza. So far in the world at the time of my filming, only sixteen had been found; they were seven inches or larger and in good condition.

I flew into Wilmington, rented a car, and drove north to Morehead City to do a week of wreck diving. Here I got to dive several wrecks on the bottom of the ocean, often referred to as the "Graveyard of the Atlantic." I enjoyed interviewing Captain George Purifoy and his friend, Claude Hull, about their finding the German submarine lying just forty miles off the North Carolina coast. It was amazing to think that during the war, the Germans were that close to the USA when the Americans sank the sub. Shortly after the show was produced and sent to their dive shop where I had made the film, I heard the sad news that George had died in a diving accident. The family contacted me, requesting some extra copies, since my interview with George was the last interview the family had of him on DVD. I was honored to have met him and to be able to supply their last request.

One of the highlights for me was a dive trip on the way back to Wilmington, North Carolina, when I again went out on a dive boat forty miles into the ocean to a place that used to be the original shoreline of the Atlantic. This was before the ice age moved the water inland forty miles. It was the original beach that extended out for as many miles, where whale bones, shark teeth, and other debris had gathered on the shoreline many years ago during the prehistoric and ice ages. The only difference was that it now lay on the ocean bottom in one-hundred-feet-deep water. Thinking about these huge sharks gave me bad thoughts of those giant dinosaurs that must have roamed the area seas at the time. Many of the sharks alive during the time of the megalodon are still around today.

The megalodon was a predecessor to the great white shark, but by its sheer size, it would make today's great white shark look like a toy poodle in comparison. These were giant creatures from the past, and apparently once the dinosaurs died on the planet, having lost their main food supply, the megalodon also perished from the oceans. It is theorized that large animals such as the dinosaurs died either from some kind of natural cause or from the great flood, as explained in the Bible. Either way, these giant megalodons, which roamed the oceans, died because mammals this size required a huge food supply, and they might have found tough times when food was scarce. Anyway, it is a good thing they all vanished, since we divers certainly wouldn't be swimming and diving in today's oceans if they still existed.

These were behemoth, fifty- to sixty-foot eating machines. I was so impressed that, on just two dives, I was able to surface with about a dozen teeth, two of which were over five inches long and three inches wide. You can still find them in a variety of sizes on the ocean floor. I take them into classrooms with me today to show kids and adults just what it's like to hold these giant, heavy-as-iron teeth, which still have their serrated cutting edges intact along the edges of the teeth. To hold these very heavy teeth in your hands and realize they came from a living shark from the dinosaur past is, for most people, hard to fathom. It was fun searching for the teeth, but it was definitely a dive made for advanced divers, not for the beginning diver, since the depths to get down to the shoreline itself are one hundred feet and more. At that depth, your bottom time is limited, since you can stay at this depth for only around fifteen minutes at a time. I had to work quickly to search for the teeth, then return to the dive boat.

The teeth have been preserved in limestone rock over the years, and over time the limestone has disintegrated, allowing the teeth to fall out and lie on the sandy beach bottom. On my first dive, I had no idea what they looked like, so the divemaster showed me one he had found, which became mine. It looks like a piece of red, rusty steel under the water. Once my eyes adjusted to looking for them, it was easier to find them in the treasure search. I guess I tend to think of it like searching for mushrooms. On the farm when I was a kid, we went out into the woods to look for mushrooms, and each season the hunt took a while before I found my first one and got my eyes used to identifying one to find large quantities. To me this was just like searching for the teeth.

Once I got down on the bottom at one hundred feet, I needed to have a tagline attached to me and back to the boat's anchor before going out on the search to the ocean floor. With everyone digging in the sand, looking for teeth, the bottom water became very cloudy with silt—so much so that I might have gotten lost and not even been able to see where the boat was located. We also carried collection bags on our weight belts, canvas bags for items once we found them, so we didn't lose our treasures.

I watched my dive computer. When it warned me it was time to go up, I surfaced and did my safety stop at the fifteen-foot level for three minutes; even longer if I was running late and didn't get up in time. We then took an hour or more break, having lunch on the boat, then prepared to go down for our second and final dive of the day. It took two hours to travel out the forty miles to the shoreline and took the same amount of time to get back, so with that and the two dives, the trip pretty much shot the entire day—and all for a total of thirty minutes of dive time on the bottom of the ocean. Oh, but it was fun and worth it for sure.

Some guys on the boat were regular weekly divers, searching for that special tooth that could bring them as much as twenty thousand dollars, so it really was a search for treasure. The largest tooth found on our trip was found by a first-time diver at that location. Like mine, it measured just over six inches. A picture appears at the end of this book of that exact tooth as well as a picture of the teeth I found. I filmed the entire experience, and it appears at the end of the North Carolina wreck diving show. If I had a chance to do this trip again, I would. It was one of the most enjoyable experiences I ever had while diving.

Newly found megalodon tooth off North Carolina before it was cleaned

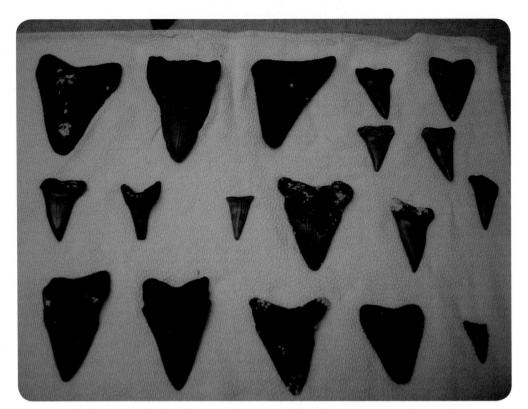

Megalodon teeth found on my dive trip off Wilmington, North Carolina

Chapter 21

Back Home Again in Michigan

Shortly after making the North Carolina show, I was somewhat shamed into making a show on my home state of Michigan. Divers said, "You have made all these shows so far, yet you haven't even produced one on your own home state of Michigan." I thought about It, and I had to agree with them, so I needed to get started on a plan. I spent the summer of 2008 trying to come up with a plan with dive shops in northern Michigan and the Upper Peninsula, and I finally got it all together.

By August, I was ready to begin filming, which took me a few trips to complete in the fall of the year, since the leaves were just starting to change color after Labor Day. I know what you are thinking. *By then the water is cold.* The answer is no; it is by that time of year—the end of summer—that the water is the warmest the Great Lakes ever get. It takes all summer to begin to warm them up; by late fall they are at their peak temps before dropping drastically in the winter. Lake-effect snow is produced during cooler atmospheric conditions when a cold air mass moves across long expanses of warmer lake water, sometimes causing huge amounts of snow just as late fall and early winter begin.

Show 18: *Shipwrecks of the Upper Great Lakes of Michigan* (Filmed in August 2008)

This show became our biggest-selling DVD of them all. We distributed it throughout northern Michigan to various gift shops in Mackinaw City, on Mackinac Island, and in the Upper Peninsula, where it became one of the take-home souvenirs of our state.

The DVD box cover reads as follows:

> We are in our home state of Michigan for this edition of *Dive Travel.* Many have asked us to dive and explore a few of the many hundreds of shipwrecks in the northern part of our Great Lakes. On this show, we visit eight shipwrecks. Two in Lake Michigan: the SS *Eber Ward*, sunk in 1909; and the *Sandusky*, sunk in 1856, prior to the Civil War. We visit two in Lake Huron: the *Cedarville*, the third-largest shipwreck in the Great Lakes, sunk in 1965; and the *William Barnum*, sunk in 1894. In Lake Superior, just off Munising, we visit four: the *Steven M. Selvick, a* seventy-one-foot "city class" tugboat; the *Herman H. Nettles,* a two-hundred-foot steam barge with three masts; the *Smith Moore,* a two-hundred-twenty-six-foot, wooden-hulled steamer; and the *Bermuda,* a one-hundred forty-five-foot schooner.
>
> The Lower Peninsula is connected to the Upper Peninsula of Michigan by way of the mighty Mackinac Bridge, built in 1957 as the world's longest suspension bridge at five miles long. Today it still holds the title as the third longest in the world. Topside we tour Mackinaw City, St. Ignace, and Mackinac Island, where the Hollywood movie *Somewhere in Time* was filmed. We take an

exciting open-air biplane flight over the mighty Mackinac Bridge and the Straits of Mackinac Underwater Preserve. Later, we visit Sault Sainte Marie and the world-famous Soo Locks, which we also film from a plane. We tour some of the area's historic lighthouses as well as Tahquamenon Falls, then visit the Great Lakes Shipwreck Museum at Whitefish Point on Lake Superior, take a boat ride on a glass-bottom boat to see wrecks from the surface, and finally take a breathtaking sunset cruise along the famous Pictured Rocks National Shoreline.

It took me a few trips up and back to get all this accomplished. I opened the show standing in front of the famous iconic Mackinac Bridge on the shore off Mackinaw City with my camera facing north. Interestingly the spelling of the names *Mackinaw* and *Mackinac* is different and can be confusing. If you are talking about Mackinaw City, which is the city on the south end of the bridge and the gateway to the north, it is spelled just as I wrote it— Mackinaw. But if you are talking about the bridge itself, it is spelled Mackinac Bridge, just as it is with Mackinac Island, even though the vast majority pronounce them the same way—Mackinaw.

I filmed topside over a few days, and one of the most exciting parts was my flight in a biplane over the bridge. It was a dream come true; I enjoyed it so much. I ended up taking two more flights with others who I thought might enjoy experiencing this incredible adventure—my close friend, Bill, and later my oldest grandson. It was surely a once-in-a-lifetime opportunity.

While diving the *Cedarville*, located just east of the bridge, our first attempt had to be abandoned since the waves and currents were so strong after getting out of the boat. We couldn't even reach the bottom to begin filming, especially while carrying my heavy camera. We had on board with me that day a group of technical divers; even they had to turn back due to the poor weather. On the Great Lakes, weather can change in an instant; I have seen it happen. One can go out to sea on a relatively clear day or with partly cloudy skies and go down diving, only to come up in a pouring-down rainstorm in just a matter of an hour. The common joke in Michigan is, if you don't like the weather, wait a few minutes.

This reminds me of the time in Cadillac, Michigan, when our dive shop owner, Morris, along with me and two other dive buddies from our dive shop, Gene and Tim, went up to the Straits of Mackinac one weekend just a year earlier in late fall (October or early November). It turned into being a very strange and scary weekend we would each long remember. I even refer to it as the "twilight zone experience." Let me explain.

We were all divemasters and above at the time, along with Morris, a PADI course director. We went up on a Saturday morning, not arriving until late morning. Our driver, Tim, who was pulling his boat, ran out of gas just as we got to the St. Ignace turnoff and our destination. That problem should have been a red-flag warning for what lay ahead of us for the weekend. We had to walk to a gas station and get gas to continue our journey.

Once we finally launched the boat and were in the rough waters off the straits that weekend, the winds howled, and I ended up losing my cherished *Dive Travel* hat, which had a lot of dive pins on it from my travels around the world. Suddenly it was in the water, having blown off my head from the fierce winds, and was gone forever in the straits just off the Mackinac Bridge.

Morris had made an agreement with the local dive shop in St. Ignace that weekend to pull all the buoys off the shipwrecks we planned to dive to here in the Great Lakes following our final dives for the season on the wrecks that weekend. We were the last to dive those wrecks before winter. The shop in St. Ignace was responsible for both putting in and taking out all the buoys for that region of the straits. These buoy markers are attached to all the shipwrecks each season so dive boats can find them and anchor to them with ease during the summer season.

By now the waters were starting to turn cold and rough, and we all had our dry suits on to combat the cold temps below. Some wear dry suits in the Great Lakes year around. After diving, filming, and pulling buoys the rest of Saturday afternoon, it was time to head to our motel for the night. It was cold and rainy, and we were all wet and hungry—ready to get in some warm, dry clothes and get something to eat.

The next day we went out to finish our dives and collect the remaining buoys attached to the last wrecks we planned to dive. Again, it was windy. Gene and I tried to put on our dry suits in the boat on the way out and ended up getting wet, bounding around on the boat as it crossed the waves, and getting cold water in our what-were-supposed-to-be dry suits.

On the way out, suddenly the boat engine died, and we were afloat in the wind. Tim, our captain, tried repeatedly to get it started. We were in the process of calling the Coast Guard for a possible rescue, but suddenly the engine started, and we were off, not knowing whether the engine would suddenly die once more.

Finally, we had made it west of the bridge at the wreck site of the *Sandusky*, a wooden schooner, sunk in 1856, prior to the Civil War. Seven sailors had died in that shipwreck on a cold November day while coming across Lake Michigan from Chicago. An interesting side note: the seven men who died had been in jail in Chicago at the time of the big Chicago fire, and the sheriff had released them, not knowing he was sending them to their deaths.

We anchored at the buoy; and Gene, Morris, and I went down first to tour the ship and film it, while Tim stayed topside. Later, the three of us came back up and rested. Tim then got ready to take his turn to go down, and Morris got his tools ready to take down and prepare to disconnect the buoy. Tim made it down and was on the wreck below, while Morris got in the water after getting a wrench with which to unlatch the buoy. But suddenly he somehow lost hold of the boat and began drifting in back of us, slowly being blown by the wind across the water. We couldn't reach him, even after throwing a rescue tube and towline to him.

Gene, who was also a captain, decided to unhook from the wreck buoy, even though we had a diver below on the wreck, and leave him long enough to capture Morris before he ended up lost in the Great Lakes out to sea. The boat at first didn't want to start again, but suddenly the engine started—praise the Lord!—and we motored over to Morris. He grabbed hold of the boat and held on as we dragged him slowly back to where the buoy held onto the wreck below with its lone diver.

By the time we reached the ship and buoy, Morris was out of breath from holding on. It made for a scary time for us all. Finally, Tim surfaced, not knowing that we had left him. They went back down together and released the chain to the buoy so we could pull it in and get out of there. By this time, we were all extremely cold, wet, exhausted, and certainly ready to get warm, have dinner, and finally be free from our strange weekend of diving. This experience just goes to show how quickly things can and do sometimes go wrong on a dive when least expected, even with experienced divers.

I had a similar experience happen to me once on a dive in the ocean. I'm not even sure where it was in the world, but I remember coming up to what was supposed to be the buoy; and after doing my safety stop, I came up to find the end of the rope attached to nothing. The boat was gone and nowhere in sight. I wasn't alone, however; there were a couple of divers floating on the surface, and soon the boat came back to get us. But it was a very strange feeling to surface and find that my boat ride home had disappeared.

Finally, in continuing to film my Michigan show, I returned on a weekend when the weather was much better and sunny. It was just me and the dive boat's captain, who went down and filmed the *Cedarville* shipwreck on the east side of the Mackinac Bridge. The view looked very spooky from down below when looking at the massive five-hundred-eighty-eight-foot ship and peering into the windows located on the ship's second floor.

I had earlier interviewed the son of one of the ship's survivors, and he had informed me that ten of the crew of thirty men had lost their lives by going down with the ship after it collided with a Norwegian ship in a heavy fog in May 1965. Anyway, the site felt eerie to me, more than with other shipwrecks I had dived. It almost appeared as though someone was watching us, making me shiver at the thought, and I wanted to get out, or maybe it was just the cold water at forty-four degrees in the one-hundred-foot-deep water. But this is precisely why I had bought a dry suit; at least it kept me dry from the water—as long as I didn't try putting it on while on a moving vessel. For dry-suit diving, you even need to take a PADI dry-suit dive course just for that alone.

On Mackinac Island, it was fun filming all the horse-drawn carriages. I was on such a carriage, filming as it left the famous Grand Hotel, and ventured below, making great video on the way down the hill, along with great audio, too, as the horses clip-clopped down the street, pulling our buggy. I was also given permission to film the beautiful gardens on the grounds below the stairs in front of the massive Grand Hotel.

Later in Sault Sainte Marie, I got in a plane and flew over the Soo Locks. I had a bird's-eye view of the famous locks below, seeing the navigation of the ships entering and leaving the Saint Mary's River as they travel from one Great Lake to another. I had been told that the largest active ship in the Great Lakes at the time was the *Paul R. Tregurtha*, at one thousand and thirteen feet, known as the Queen of the Lakes. That ship was getting close to arriving at the locks; my prayers were answered. I had a little time, so I drove quickly down to the Saint Mary's River, located south of town near the *Sugar Island Ferry*, and got video of the massive ship as it arrived in the Saint Mary's River, passing me by at a very close range. It was great for filming it from the river leading upstream to the locks. My plan was to hurry back to the airport, where I had lined up a small, two-seat, private plane to take me up and follow the ship as it came into the locks. It all worked perfectly with timing in the best arrangement I had made to date, thanks to a little help from above and to the woman who worked at the locks and tipped me off with some ideas about filming it.

All in all, I spent about three weeks, back and forth, filming the entire area where the show was featured, from Mackinaw City to Sault Sainte Marie and from Whitefish Point to Pictured Rocks in Munising. Finally, we had a finished show from the Great Lakes State of Michigan called *Shipwrecks of the Upper Great Lakes of Michigan*.

One of the questions I always get about Michigan is, did you ever get to dive the wreck of the famous *Edmond Fitzgerald*? Well, the answer is no, and I will explain why. The *Edmond Fitzgerald* was the largest ship on the Great Lakes at the time of its mysterious sinking November 10, 1975, in a Lake Superior storm. There were almost hurricane-force winds and thirty-five-foot waves, with the loss of the entire crew of twenty-nine. It sank seventeen miles north-northwest of Whitefish Point in Michigan's Upper Peninsula. Even a song sung by Gordon Lightfoot was dedicated and made famous honoring that ship. The song's phrase "The lake it is said, never gives up her dead" refers to the extremely cold conditions and depths of Superior, the largest of the Great Lakes.

The *Fitzgerald*, a bulk cargo- and ore-carrying vessel, was seven hundred twenty-eight feet long. Today several such vessels are over one thousand feet in length. But at the time, it was the queen, the largest and one of the newest ships to ply the waters of the Great Lakes. Like the *Titanic*, it was considered almost unsinkable, being a fairly new ship. It is now listed as the largest shipwreck in the Great Lakes today. She sank in Canadian Ontario waters, broke in half, and still rests at the bottom of that location in about five hundred thirty feet of water. The deepest spot in Lake Superior, however, is one thousand three hundred thirty-two feet at a location near Munising, Michigan.

Three factors keep divers from diving the wreck. One, it is in Canadian waters, where permission isn't granted. Two, at the depth of five hundred thirty feet, no recreational diver can dive that deep, although in the early days some technical divers did dive it. Later, due to its depth, a submarine filmed it to try and determine what had caused it to sink. Third, and most importantly, it is considered a memorial burial site, for all the bodies still entombed inside the wreck are preserved by the cold, deep waters of Lake Superior.

There have been countless thousands of shipwrecks in all the Great Lakes, taking with them many thousands of lives. Strange also is the fact that most wrecks occurred in the month of November, when raging storms brew in the middle of the Great Lakes as winter approaches. Storms will approach, it seems, out of nowhere. Only Mother Nature controls the seasons. If you want to know more, there are many fascinating books available at the library on shipwrecks located in all the Great Lakes.

It was soon after this release of the Michigan show that I started to get interested in selling our small collection of DVDs we had produced thus far. I had bought a covered, enclosed trailer; we had it covered in decals displaying our dive shows to advertise the series. Our first exhibition show we attended was "Our World Underwater," the annual dive show held each year in Chicago. Of course, to attend we had to sign up months in advance, or it would be sold out with exhibitors. My son-in-law drove and went out there with me; we bought a booth, set up our tables with a giant TV in the back of the booth, and showed our DVD promos during the three-day show. We sold a lot of DVDs, but no matter how many we sold, by the time we paid for the booth, the cost of driving from Michigan, hotels, and food, all we did was break even. But I thought perhaps just the advertising alone would pay for itself with later sales from our website.

My son-in-law and me at our first Dive Travel booth at a show in Chicago

We branched out more the next year. We also attended a second exhibition show called "Beneath the Sea" in New Jersey just outside of New York City. It was a larger show, but again we just broke even. You had to sell a lot of DVDs, and we did sell a lot. In one of the last years we exhibited, we also included a third show and went to DEMA, the largest dive exhibition in the country, held in Orlando, Florida. Again, we managed to break even, though we never did make any money over and above the cost involved, but we sold thousands of DVDs over the years. Divers stopped by our booth and picked out the dive travelogues they were interested in attending in future dive trips to give them a preview of what to expect from various locations of the world, helping them to decide on a future vacation trip.

DVDs packaged at our booth a few years later at DEMA in Orlando, Florida

In addition, my DVDs were now being spread all over the world. Each dive shop of the countries I had filmed in were sent free copies, per our agreement, for their hosting me. They either sold or gave away the copies for their own promotion in every country I visited. It was at these DEMA shows where I got to meet up with people from all the destinations I had previously filmed and brought DVDs to. It was so much fun and was always like a worldwide family reunion of sorts—meeting all the dive-shop owners and employees I had been with over the years from all those destinations, and meeting others from all the future destinations I would soon be with. The experience reminds me of these words I live by, which are hanging on my wall at home: "There will always be a reason why you meet people, either you need them to change your life, or you're the one that will change theirs."

Shipwrecks of the Upper Great Lakes of Michigan box cover

Chapter 22

Welcome to Diving in Asia with Volcanoes in the Ring of Fire

At a DEMA show in the fall of 2008, I was invited to come aboard another liveaboard dive boat, this time in Indonesia. This would be my third boat to live on for ten days. In all my dives, I ended up living on over a dozen such boats; almost one-third of all my shows were made from boats at sea, where I literally did nothing but eat, sleep, and dive 24/7, making a minimum of five dives a day or one every couple of hours. After about a week of this, or even ten days of it, I was more than ready to get off the boat and back onto land.

Finally, in November 2008, I flew to Manado in North Sulawesi, Indonesia, to begin work on show number nineteen. That would take up to three weeks to film, a week touring the countryside, then the rest of the time on the *Ocean Rover*, our host boat.

Our dive boat, the Ocean Rover, off in the distance in Indonesia

Show 19: *Manado, North Sulawesi, Indonesia* **(Filmed in November 2008)**

Join us on this special one-hour edition of *Dive Travel* as we take you to Manado, the capital city of North Sulawesi, Indonesia. Upon arrival, we stay at the Cocotinos Resort (www.cocotinos.com) and Odyssea Divers, a small beach resort in picturesque Wori Bay, North Sulawesi, in the heart of Kima Bajo (a fishing village) overlooking Bunaken National Marine Park just twenty minutes from the Manado airport. We spend three weeks touring the area, including twelve days of diving on board the luxury dive boat *Ocean Rover* out at sea. During this time, we make forty dives from Manado north to Sangihe Island. Included in our travel are Lembeh Strait, Biaro Island, Ruang and Tagulandang Islands, Siau Island, Para Island, Mehengetang Island (an underwater volcano), Kahakitang Island, Bangka Island, Pulisan (on the mainland), Bunaken National Marine Park, the Minahasa area, and Poopo. This is a paradise for macro enthusiasts and still photographers, with an incredible array of fascinating macro marine life found on what is known as "muck dives," which captivate all divers' interests. We also visit an active underwater volcano and witness its hot stream of warm bubbles rising to the surface from the hot rocks. We visit the famous hot springs, tour an inland sulfur-filled lake that changes colors, and walk through the lush foliage and deep, humid Indonesian jungle, where we approach a tribe of native Celebes crested black macaque monkeys, found on only two islands here. In addition, we visit a tree housing the tarsier monkeys, the smallest monkeys on the planet. Plus, we visit local markets, historic cemeteries, vegetable farmlands, rice fields, and fish farms along the way, while viewing the beautiful rolling countryside. We also find farmers with oxen pulling old, wooden carts along the rural roads. It is just as picturesque as you might imagine, and all is located on the opposite side of the planet.

Truly, this is a jam-packed show filled with all sorts of neat things I was ready to explore. This land, far away from modern civilization, was located in the back country and surrounded by volcanic mountains. It made for a pictorial background among its native residents. There was so much to see in the three weeks we had scheduled. I found it to be one of the most beautiful countries I had ever been in, and this soon became one of my favorite shows to film of all time. I had to take so many flights just to reach Manado: from the USA to Japan, to Singapore, to Jakarta, and then to Manado. It almost outranked my trip to Australia. In fact, in a later show from Indonesia, it was longer than my trip to Australia. But in this country, I felt like a foreigner more than in any other country I had been to.

The show opens with me surrounded by a group of local native children, who lived in nearby Kima Bajo, all standing on the beach. They were so cute, innocent, and poor. I saw them playing along the beach each day and became friendly with them. So I invited them to be on camera in my show, and that was all it took; I was immediately surrounded by these beautiful children as word spread among them that they could be on TV. I had gone into town earlier and purchased some bags of candy to pass out to the village children as a thank-you when we finished filming the opening and closing shots.

Native children dancers, standing with me on one of my trips to Indonesia

These children of God were so precious to me. I remember thinking at the time how so many I had read about earlier had been tragically killed in raging storms, typhoons, and tsunami tidal waves. These weather events could take over in an instant in the various parts of these exotic islands of this Asian country. What amazed me was that most of the island residents didn't go into the water that much, and sadly few knew how to swim. This fact led me to do some research, which follows.

We all know that seventy-one percent of the earth is covered by oceans or fresh water, leaving twenty-nine percent as land mass, and of that only ten percent is inhabited by humans. Well then, with so much water surrounding us, wouldn't you think it would be a responsibility to teach everyone how to swim for survival? We don't even do that here in the USA. According to the World Health Organization, there are an estimated three hundred seventy-two thousand deaths by drowning each year worldwide. In fact, it is the third-leading cause of unintentional injury deaths or seven percent of all injury-related deaths globally.

Ten Americans drown each day in the USA alone. If you are wondering what the second-leading cause of unintentional injury deaths is, it is falls; four hundred twenty-four thousand die each year globally from falling. And the number one leading cause of death is from injuries, violence, and traffic deaths worldwide. So there you have it. Over four billion of the seven billion people living on this planet cannot swim (or less than forty-two percent of the world population can swim). Even worse, more than one-half of Americans cannot swim. So now you know how sad I felt for these children's well-being, not being prepared to swim in the very extreme possibility of a storm, typhoon, or tsunami hitting these small islands, which house many of these families, who live only in shacks and grass-roofed homes.

Over in these Asian countries, they refer to storms as typhoons. We, on the other hand, call them hurricanes; they are both the same. But recently, these typhoons are becoming more and more powerful. One of the last to hit the Philippines was the most powerful storm to ever hit anywhere in the world on planet earth; the devastation was immense, killing over six thousand natives living in its path.

Roman, the owner of the *Ocean Rover*, also the captain, got along with me right away. He, along with his second mate, personally escorted me around the countryside for a week prior to boarding the ship. They had asked me to come a week early so we could film the area in advance and then spend another week after the boat dives to film even more topography. That was why I had to schedule such a long trip there. We drove to volcano mountains, passed fields of farmland, and drove by oxen pulling old, wooden carts loaded with vegetables and other products. It was a priceless pictorial taken right out of an old history textbook.

One day we attended a farm market, where everyone gathered to buy and sell produce. It was huge, and I got more than I bargained for when we went inside. First, I saw fruits and vegetables—many native only to the islands, local fruits I had never seen or heard of before. But it was the meat that got me going—or should I say had me going out the door quickly. These items included roasted bats, rats, and other wild critters, including fresh-butchered dogs, lying on their backs all stiff with their legs straight up in the air. The smell of blood all over the ground from fresh butchering was nauseating, to say the least. I remember seeing a live dog inside running around, and I thought, *Get out of here now. Run for your life if you want to continue living.*

I thought long and hard about this way of life for the poor farmers and residents who lived here, and I realized it wasn't any different from home in my early years while growing up on the farmland of Michigan. We used to hunt rabbits and squirrels on my farm back in the 1950s. Back then, we ate what we hunted to survive, and it was no different with these people; it was a way of survival for the inhabitants who lived in this place called Indonesia. The people were poor, and any type of meat was protein for their family. Here families lived together, with grown children taking care of their elderly parents. They had limited incomes, and most were poor, so they consumed what they could grow or hunt.

Once we got in the water and started diving, I fell in love with the underwater world in the Pacific Ocean; it was so much better diving here in the beautiful corals and extra-warm eighty-five-degree water than anything I had ever experienced in the Caribbean. I was already hooked on the Pacific Ocean and would be returning for many future trips.

Here's an update. Many years later, a tsunami occurred not far from where I had filmed this first show from Indonesia, sadly killing many island residents. This critical exotic area in the Ring of Fire is lined with volcanoes, and these are the most dangerous areas in the world to live in, from both tsunamis and typhoons, which strike the islands with horrific wind force. My heart goes out to the many people I met there, and still I wonder whether the children I filmed survived.

Here's a little about volcanoes. More than eighty percent of the earth's surface above and below sea level is made up of volcanic origin. There are about fifteen hundred potentially active volcanoes worldwide, aside from the continuous belt of volcanoes on the ocean floor. About five hundred of these have erupted in historical time. Many of these are located along the Pacific Rim, in what is known as the Ring of Fire. There are one hundred sixty-nine potentially active volcanoes in the United States alone. The United States ranks third, behind Indonesia and Japan, in the number of historically active volcanoes. Scientists estimate that about four thousand volcanoes are located per million square kilometers on the ocean floor of the Pacific Ocean (which totals three hundred sixty-one million square kilometers). Can one then even begin to comprehend just how many volcanoes could be located under the entire ocean system?

Bubbles rising from boiling water from an underwater volcano, Indonesia

There are more than a million submarine, underwater volcanoes and perhaps as many as seventy-five thousand which rise over half a mile above the ocean floor. Submarine volcanoes are vents or fissures in the earth's surface, from which magma can erupt. Many of the submarine volcanoes are located near areas of the tectonic plate movement, known as mid-ocean ridges. In the Bible, God ended the world with a flood after instructing Noah to build an ark. This next time God forewarns the world will end in fire. It certainly wouldn't take long to end the world in fire if all the volcanoes were ignited at once. The top-ten countries with the most volcanoes are the United States, with one hundred seventy-three; Russia, with one hundred sixty-six; Indonesia, with one hundred thirty-nine; Iceland, with one hundred thirty; Japan, with one hundred twelve; Chile, with one hundred four; Ethiopia, with fifty-seven; Papua New Guinea, with fifty-three; the Philippines, with fifty; and Mexico, with forty-three.

Sea anemone fish, Indonesia

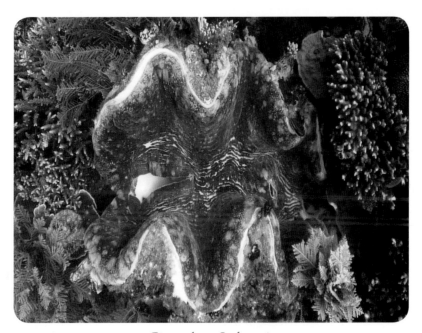

Giant clam, Indonesia

In November 2008, after attending another DEMA show, I got bookings for the most shows I would ever film in one year, almost one every month starting in January 2009. In January, I was invited to go to Nassau, the Bahamas, again, after another dive show I had attended where I had met the owner of a dive resort in Nassau, so it became our twentieth show in our series. We were now just a little over the halfway mark, which would eventually become a thirty-seven-volume library.

Show 20: *Nassau, the Bahamas* (Filmed in January 2009)

Travel with us as we visit Nassau, the capital of the Bahamas, on New Providence Island for this edition of *Dive Travel*. In 1670 British settlers came to New Providence Island and built Fort Charlestown, but in 1684 the Spanish burned it to the ground. It was later rebuilt and renamed Nassau in 1695 to Honor King William III (formerly Prince of Orange, Nassau). We dive with Stuart Cove's Aqua Adventures and visit the wrecks made famous in many Hollywood movies. With its clear waters and abundant marine life, Nassau is often hailed as "the underwater Hollywood," with such movies as *Splash*, *Flipper*, *Jaws IV*, *Speed 2*, *Into the Blue*, *Open Water*, *After the Sunset*, plus four James Bond movies, and much more.

Meanwhile on neighboring, modern Paradise Island, just a bridge crossing away, many other topside activities exist. Another small private island, known as Blue Lagoon (a three-mile trip by boat), served as the location for the beach scenes in the movie *Splash*. It was here that we visited Dolphin Encounters, home to eighteen Atlantic bottlenose dolphins, including the internationally famous "Flipper." We interview their staff of instructors about the marine life they offered for those special encounters, including Murray, the famous sea lion. In September 2006, Dolphin Encounters became the permanent home to six California sea lions displaced from Gulfport, Mississippi, after Hurricane Katrina. Several of the famous sea lions appeared in such movies as *Andre* and *Slappy and the Stinkers*.

For the show's opening, I stood with two parrots on my shoulder at Stuart's Cove. Later I stood with one of the stars of the show at Blue Lagoon, Murray, the famous sea lion who starred in the Hollywood movie, *Slappy and the Stinkers*. He was twenty years old at the time and smarter than I was; it took me four tries to get my lines right. He was a real show-off and was always on cue. I got a chance to spend some fun quality time with him in the pool, where he interacted with me by doing tricks in the show.

Murray, the famous sea lion, with me at a show opening at Dolphin Encounters, Nassau, Bahamas

At Stuart's Cove, I interviewed Stuart, the owner of the dive shop, one of the largest and most successful dive operations in the world. He was our main host for the show on the main island of Nassau. Stuart even assigned a dive master, Liz, who was also the dive shop's talented model and my dive buddy, to do the show's dive tip of the week. As a model for Stuart's Cove, she was in most of the scenes I filmed. Underwater, I filmed Liz in a very attractive and colorful pink-and-blue custom dive suit. It was funny meeting her here, since I had met her earlier as our divemaster onboard our dive boat at the Turks and Caicos Islands, when we filmed that previous show, where she then had worked.

I find It interesting to see various divemasters as well as captains of ships moving around to various regions of the world. I had another divemaster on my show in Costa Rica, only to find him a couple of years later on a dive boat at Cocos Island. I had a former captain of my show on the great white sharks off Guadalupe Island, Mexico, whom I later found as the captain on another dive boat in the Sea of Cortez. It is always fun to catch up with them and find out the latest dive industry gossip.

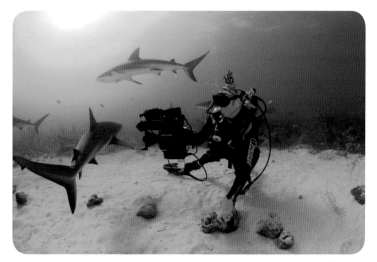

Surrounded by sharks on the bottom of the Caribbean off Nassau

Stuart's Cove Aqua Adventures, Bahamas, taking pictures with more sharks

On a reef filming with lights on my camera system

Chapter 23

Giant Pacific Mantas

Show twenty-one was made after I returned from a DEMA show and made contacts with the *Nautilus Explorer* crew. This was one of two shows I filmed on this beautiful dive boat, the second one being later in Alaska aboard the same craft.

Show 21: *Revillagigedo Archipelago, Mexico* (Filmed in February 2009)

On this *Dive Travel* adventure, we visit three of the four volcanic islands making up the Revillagigedo Archipelago two hundred fifty miles off the southern coast of Cabo San Lucas, Mexico, in the Pacific Ocean. It is here that we encounter the magnificent, giant Pacific manta rays (Manta Birostris), the largest of the rays. These beautiful mantas love swimming and interacting with humans as much as humans love interacting with them. These gentle giants of the sea have wingspans of up to seven point six meters or twenty-five feet across and can weigh approximately twenty-three hundred kilograms or twenty-five hundred to five thousand pounds. We fly into San José Del Cabo, rent a car, and drive nearly forty minutes across the lonely, cactus-filled desert, seldom ever seeing another car. Eventually we arrive at Cabo San Lucas, a lively resort town nestled on the southern tip of the Baja California Peninsula, overlooking the Sea of Cortez. Here we tour the town and the topside scenery and take a flight on an ultralight plane as it soars over the resort town and the famous rock arch, as well as the marina and cruise ships lined up at port. A boat ride around the beaches reveals sea lions sunning themselves on the rocky beach areas near the famous arch. Here we dive with the sea lions. Later we finally board the luxury dive boat *Nautilus Explorer* for an eight-day diving adventure two hundred fifty miles south of the mainland. It is here that we find the giant mantas, hammerhead sharks, and a variety of other sharks and marine life. The beautiful, rocky volcanic pinnacles sticking up from the ocean floor make up the Revillagigedo Archipelago Islands of Socorro, San Benedicto, and Roca Partida. We also witness humpback whales occasionally rising to the surface during their annual pilgrimage. Sit back and enjoy this incredible, stunning video from the Sea of Cortez and the Pacific Ocean off Mexico.

Again, we were on another liveaboard vessel. Of the thirty-seven shows I made, ten of the shows were on liveaboards, where I spent anywhere from on average of seven to ten days on board, some up to three weeks. I often felt more at home in the ocean than I did on the boats. We averaged five dives every day when we were on the boats, approximately an hour each dive, so you can imagine how many hours and dives I did over the years, and that was just on the liveaboards.

This show was very special; I loved interacting with the giant mantas, which followed us everywhere like puppy dogs. They loved our attention, mainly because they loved the feel of our dive bubbles brushing the outer skin under their bodies. I am sure for them it felt like being in a bubbling Jacuzzi. They swam over the top of us many times over and over—quite close to our heads, too—to get that hard-bubbling effect under their vast bodies.

Giant Pacific manta off Revillagigedos Archipelagos, Mexico

This is about the only place in the world where you will find this large of a manta. Sometimes they startled us, too, since these creatures weighed as much as a ton with their gigantic, twenty-five-foot wingspan. Divers in their midst looked very small in comparison. It was like a giant bird in the sky or having an airplane pass a matter of inches over your head as it constantly made dives, swooping around us. The rays loved us so much that they even continued to follow our dive boat to the next island destination, not wanting to see us leave. I was told to stay clear of their massive flapping wings, since they could easily break your arm if you were struck by one of these big guys in the water. Other than that, they aren't a danger to humans; they don't sting you, unlike smaller southern stingrays, which are more predominate in the ocean. You really get a better idea of their size by watching them in the show.

In early 2009, I was invited to go to the Philippines to film a show for a dive shop there that was inviting a group of dive shops from the USA along with photographers on an all-expense-paid trip to promote their new dive destination. The trip included airfare, hotel, food, and travel to the area by tour bus. All I had to pay for was my flight from Michigan to San Francisco to join the tour, so again I was off as a representative of our dive shop in Cadillac, Michigan.

Show 22: *Anilao, Mabini, and Batangas, Philippines* **(Filmed in March 2009)**

> Join us as ActiVentures Adventure Tours takes us to the Philippines for an incredible eight-day dive adventure tour. We depart San Francisco on Philippine Airlines for this unusual twelve-hour nonstop direct flight to Manila. We arrive and quickly depart Manila by tour bus to Anilao, Mabini, and Batangas, about two hours south, billed as the birthplace of Philippine scuba diving and home to their most vibrant reefs and diverse marine life. It is also considered the nudibranch capital of the Philippines.

> The municipality of Mabini is more popular to tourists than Anilao. A 2003 survey by coral taxonomist Douglas Fenner listed a total of three hundred nineteen species and seventy-four genera of hard corals, including the discovery of eight rare coral species and twenty-five percent more than the average number of corals found in the hotbed known as the Coral Triangle, the rich waters shared

by Malaysia, Indonesia, and the Philippines, also referred to as the Ring of Fire. Two hundred and sixty-two species of fish were surveyed in Balayan Bay, where Mabini is located. We stop along the way by bus for breakfast and a view of the Tagaytay Taal Volcano, right outside the window. (An update later in the year 2020: This volcano exploded with ash covering an area forty miles away from the eruption.) Soon we arrive at the Acacia Resort and Dive Center, a new resort being introduced to divers by ActiVentures. The Acacia dive resort caters to divers from around the world.

On this tour, we dive the beautiful reefs and view the incredible macro marine life, including nudibranchs native to the region. Anilao is located at the far end of a small peninsula and offers over thirty-six dive sites, including steep walls, shipwrecks, and drift dives. We later dive at Puerto Galera, another popular dive site south of the capital city of Manila.

Nudibranchs are small gastropod mollusks. The name means "naked gills." They are shell-less and uncoiled gastropods, famous for their brilliant colors. There are more than three thousand known species alone. Nudibranchs are one group also informally known as sea slugs. They capture the hearts of still photographers, especially those who love to show them in a variety of pictures, some of which are stunning in a multitude of vibrant colors crawling on coral reefs below.

A nudibranch on a coral reef

Most flights I took there in later years were never direct flights but instead stopped in Japan, where we changed planes to travel on to Manila. While in the Philippines, I met a Filipino friend, Sunny, who became a local diver, and we had a lot of fun together. He offered to help me film around Manila, since he was a native of the area. So when we got back from the dives in Anilao, we spent a day touring Manila. I felt a great friendship with him; he and I hit it off right from the beginning. He spoke good English (not everyone speaks English there) and acted as my own private tour guide and interpreter when trying to find out about the local government, airport, tourist attractions, and more. It was with him that we toured the city and got all the video I needed from this very large city of over twelve million people.

In future trips for a second show, when I passed through there on my way to film other nearby countries such as Malaysia, and Indonesia, and so forth, I finally got to meet Sunny's family. His mother, sister, three brothers, plus nieces and nephews all lived under the same roof, as most Filipinos do. Like other Filipinos, not having much money, they lived in an older shack, referred to by the Filipinos as a barung-barong, located out in the countryside. I felt sorry for him and his family, especially when he later told me his roof was leaking on top of the only computer he owned. He had dreamed of going to college to become a computer engineer, but his dad had died when he was young, and he had to drop out of school and go to work to help support the family. He could no longer afford to go to college. In the Philippines at the time, the average wage was around one hundred forty dollars a month. Americans, on the other hand, could live there like a very wealthy person on just a normal wage earned back home in America.

We rented a car once, and I drove through Manila at night, but it was only due to Sunny and God guiding me on the right roads through the city. Anyone who has been there knows how scary driving can be in the city of over twelve million people with few stoplights. I have to laugh at people in LA and New York or other large cities here who talk about how bad traffic is; they have no idea what traffic is until they try to drive there in end-to-end traffic with motorcycles on all sides of them whizzing by, and when they come to an intersection, the plan is just to shove and go at one's own risk. I had to pinch myself to remind me I was driving there.

In recent years the traffic there has improved, with more stoplights being added. When I arrived back in the States, Sunny and I kept in contact, and I learned a lot about him, his family, and the Philippine lifestyle. I found Filipinos to be some of the nicest and friendliest people on the planet. They are hardworking, and many work abroad in hotels and other businesses, sending most of their hard-earned money back as support for their families in the Philippines.

I had thought about buying a condo over there so I would have a place to stay since I had many shows to film in that region, but I thought it would be selfish of me to buy a condo that I would use only once a year, while they had nothing, so I talked with him about building them a house, one I could also use when I went there. I couldn't physically own the house or land since I'm not Filipino, so we put the house in his name. Sunny and I had it built, and he managed the building account. He was very good at accounting since he worked at the time for an office-supply warehouse and did the books for them among other things. So in the end I ended up getting them a house he and his family could reside in in a safe, gated community near where he wanted to go to school. I also later sent him to college.

Picture of the house we had built

Now when I say "college," it sounds expensive, but it's just the opposite; the cost is very cheap there compared to college in our country. For example, a semester of college there is about six hundred to a thousand dollars. I am proud of him; he became almost like a son to me. He graduated years ago with a bachelor's degree in computer engineering. I can always see in his mom's misty eyes the gratitude and appreciation she emulates every time I visit for having built them a safe home. But I am the one who is truly blessed. It felt so good for me to be able to do this for him and his family.

As Jesus says in the Bible, in Acts 20:35, "I have shown you all things, how that so laboring ye ought to support the weak, and to remember the words of the Lord Jesus, how he said, It is more blessed to give than to receive." Now I would have a place to stay, my own room, and they would even safely pick me up from the airport when I arrived. This house would take a couple of years to build, so it wasn't available right away. Best of all, the house is about two hours or less from some of the best diving in the world in the Philippines. Still today I have a home away from home on the other side of the planet, whenever I want to visit, and a second family who have become very close to me. We continue to keep in touch almost daily on Skype.

Show 23: *Curaçao* (Filmed in April 2009)

Since the last DEMA show, I had been filming practically nonstop and still had four more different locations in 2009 to go—one a month for three months in a row (in April, May, and June). One was to Curaçao, one to the US Virgin Islands, and one to Alaska, followed by one back to Indonesia in November of the same year. The first was to Curaçao to make our next show for a dive shop that was the predominate dive shop on the island at the time. Remember the ABC islands I talked about before? Well, we were back again to film in April 2009.

> Welcome to colorful, picturesque Curaçao, the ABC Netherlands Antilles, the three islands made up of Aruba, Bonaire, and Curaçao. The Island of Curaçao was discovered in 1499 by Alonso de Ojeda, one of Columbus's lieutenants. The inhabitants were Indians of huge physical proportions, therefore, aptly called "Isle de los Gigantes" (or Islands of the Giants). Within twenty years, the name Curaçao appeared on a Portuguese map. The island remained Spanish until the Dutch conquered it in 1643. I fly from Miami to Curaçao for the eight-day tour of one of the most colorful islands ever. All the buildings on the island are painted in bright pastel colors, giving the towns and countryside a vibrant coloration. It is a cruise ship destination, bringing travelers in from around the world to visit its historic UNESCO town center and topside attractions, such as the Sea Aquarium, the Dolphin Academy, and the Kura Hulanda Natural History Museum, plus loads of shopping, and various island tours. Our dive host is Ocean Encounters Diving, a PADI, five-star dive resort. The hotels we will be visiting are LionsDive Beach Resort, the Curaçao Hilton, and SuperClubs Breezes Curaçao. Just a short swim from shore, Curaçao coast is lined with spectacular world-class diving in crystal-clear water, including walls, reefs, and shipwrecks teaming with fish and covered in vibrant coral. We will be diving the Mushroom Forest, the *Superior Producer* iconic shipwreck, the Dolphin Dive, and many other world-renowned sites by boat.

The minute I arrived I was awestruck by the colorful painted buildings that really set the town off in style along the boats' harbor. It's certainly the prettiest island of the three ABC islands. While on the island, I got to visit my third of the four world dolphin training centers, which take dolphins out in the open water. The owner of the dive shop took me out on a country drive one day to see the farmland and surrounding countryside. We stopped for lunch at an ostrich farm, where I had my first ostrich sandwich. I cannot say it was my favorite thing to eat on the island, but it was an experience. It seemed the owner wasn't used to eating one either; I remember that the first one I received wasn't totally cooked, and they took it back to recook it. Meanwhile he gave me part of his sandwich while we waited, because the sandwiches were so outrageously huge; just one would have been more than enough that we could have split it. I wasn't that impressed with the taste anyway, but finally the chef arrived with an even bigger hamburger made of ostrich.

Oh my, I thought. *How are we ever going to eat all that?* I remember we both were laughing at the thought of never, ever again returning one for recooking, since they came back bigger upon their return to us. Following lunch, we got to visit the ostrich farm and see some of the fresh-hatched, cute babies and see the very large ostrich eggs. An ostrich egg weighs anywhere from three and a half to five pounds, and one egg is equal to two dozen chicken eggs. Take one home, and you have eggs for a month.

The diving was nice but typical of all the islands I had toured in the Caribbean. The Caribbean's cooler water of the Atlantic has about thirty percent of all the corals of the world and about the same thirty percent of the marine life. So each island we attended looked about the same under the ocean when diving. We rarely saw any different corals or fish, even though each destination claimed to have the best diving. But each island topside offered something unique in its own special way, featuring various attractions.

I find, however, that once you dive in the Pacific, you tend to get spoiled, since there are three times the coral and marine life having seventy percent of each in much warmer and clearer water. But then again, it's on the other side of the planet and costs more to reach that part of the world, and sometimes it's out of the price range of the average American diver, who also maybe has only a week's vacation or limited time and wants to dive somewhere closer to home. The U.S. Virgin Islands were next on the list and were filmed the next month.

Show 24: *The U.S. Virgin Islands* **(Filmed in May 2009)**

> On this *Dive Travel* adventure, we travel to the U.S. Virgin Islands of St. Thomas, St. Croix, and St. John. With the Atlantic Ocean to the north and the Caribbean Sea to the south, the U.S. Virgin Islands enjoy beautiful weather year-round. On St. Thomas Island, we are hosted and dive with Underwater Safaris and stay at the Marriott Frenchman's Reef. On St. Croix, we are the guest of Cane Bay Dive shop, and in St. John we dive with Cruz Bay Watersports and are guests of the Westin Resort and Villas. Columbus explored the Virgin Islands in 1493. They were originally inhabited by the Carib Indians. Since 1666, England has held six of the main islands. The remaining three islands (St. Croix, St. Thomas, and St. John), as well as about fifty islets, were acquired by Denmark, which named them the Danish West Indies. In 1917, the United States purchased these islands for twenty-five million dollars. Congress granted U.S. citizenship to Virgin Islanders in 1927. Tourism is the primary economic activity. Here we dive the reefs, walls, and wrecks and encounter the marine life. Topside in St. Thomas, we tour the capital city, Charlotte Amalie, and the surrounding countryside. In St. Croix we are there for Carnival, an annual festival, and tour the Whim Plantation Museum, which is made up of eighteenth-century buildings from this former sugar estate. We tour a rum factory and the island's countryside, plus we witness the start of an official Ironman race. In St. John we tour downtown Cruz Bay and the Annaberg Sugar Mills, and we drive along the white sand beaches and tour the green hills and rain forest.

Each of the dive shows I produced offers a history lesson on each location, something I'm not offering in detail here, but when you actually watch each DVD show, you will get more of the history of each location, while we zoom in with Google Earth to portray each area in the opening scenes.

The timing of my arrival in the U.S. Virgin Islands was unusually bad, in that when I arrived they were experiencing a severe visibility issue from an unusual algae bloom covering all the waters of all three islands. It was coming in from a river in Venezuela. The bloom lasted a week or more and tinted the water green practically everywhere. Unfortunately, I couldn't just leave and come back at another time, so we had to film what we could, but we made sure to get interviews with each diving staff to clarify that this wasn't the norm, since visibility is usually eighty to one hundred feet or more of very clear water.

That was one of the problems in scheduling filming; if a hurricane passed though just prior to my arriving at a location, many times visibility was affected. That, in fact, happened once to me at a location in the Philippines; we could even see the hurricane from the plane. It was passing over as we arrived. You cannot control Mother Nature, but divers who travel understand conditions aren't always perfect all the time. Weather cannot be predicted, just as a whale cannot be expected to suddenly appear, even when predicted.

I got to fly on a seaplane there for the first time. It took off from the water and landed, going out to the outer islands of St. Thomas. All three islands were very picturesque, looking like a painting as you stood on the mountains while looking down on each main town below where the bay spread out in front of you with its blue-and-turquoise water.

Chapter 24

Glaciers and Icebergs

In June, I traveled to a colder climate to work on my next dive film.

Show 25: *Alaska* (Filmed in June 2009)

I was excited to see a state I had often thought of but didn't know whether I would like to visit, not being a cold-weather person. But once I arrived, I loved the beauty our forty-ninth state offered. The box cover says it all:

> As the great glaciers of the last ice age retreated from Southeast Alaska and British Columbia, a new and beautiful land was born. In our series, we take our dry suits to the most northern route yet, heading to Vancouver, British Columbia, Canada; and we take a ten-day cruise and dive along the Inside Passage to Sitka, Alaska. In Vancouver we tour the beautiful city, take a gondola ride up Grouse Mountain, and enjoy a spectacular helicopter tour of the surrounding snow-capped mountain ranges overlooking the beautiful harbor before boarding Captain Mike's *Nautilus Explorer* on this special cruise.
>
> As we cruise the majestic one-thousand-mile Inside Passage, the ever-changing panorama of natural beauty comes alive. It is here that we witness hundreds of bald eagles feeding, nesting, and circling overhead, along with harbor seals, Alaskan brown bears, humpback whales, and sea otters. The *Nautilus Explorer* slowly glides through icebergs surrounding the ship and doesn't stop until we reach the LeConte Glacier located at the head end of LeConte Bay directly in front of us. Here we anxiously get off the boat to swim and stand on these giant ice cubes. We tour giant, cascading waterfalls and even sit in hot springs. But it's under the sea that we dive in our dry suits, diving in the thirty-eight- to forty-six-degree waters of the Emerald Sea and find the special coral, seals, and marine life that are native to the region and call this northern part of the country home. Sit back and enjoy this special *Dive Travel* adventure from our forty-ninth state, Alaska.

The *Nautilus Explorer* is the same dive boat we were on while filming the giant mantas in Mexico, so I was at least familiar with this boat and all it offered. This was a magical trip—from the helicopter ride through the snow-capped mountains, where we got a bird's-eye view of rugged terrain overlooking Vancouver, British Columbia, to the icebergs, which were beautiful, iridescent, blue, and floating in the passage like small ice islands.

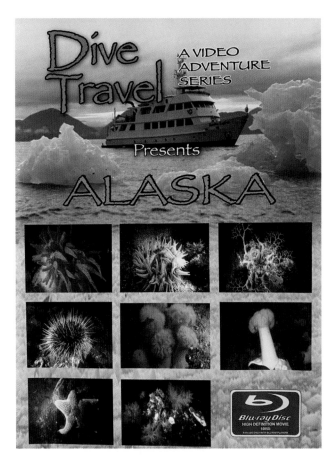

Alaska DVD cover

As we went up the Inside Passage toward Sitka, it was an unbelievable trip, revealing both the history of the area and the magnificent beauty surrounding us from every angle: snow-capped mountains, waterfalls, and green forests all sloping down to the inside river passage below. Eagles by the hundreds dotted the trees like Christmas decorations. I had never seen more than one at any one time, but here they were by the hundreds. As we drew closer to the glacier, the icebergs and smaller ice sheets, which were sometimes holding seals sitting on top, passed our boat as the theme song from *Titanic* played over the boat's speakers, giving us a real feel for the magic of the frozen area surrounding us. It was a challenge for Mike, our captain, to get the boat back to the glacier, but he did it like a pro.

Soon we were parked in front of LeConte Glacier with a mountain of ice as far as we could see in front of us. At that point, he had us get in our dive suits, get in the water, and climb up on the icebergs for a better view. It was a party breaking out as they served divers a choice of beer, wine, or hot chocolate by bringing it right out to us using a kayak. Crawling up on the ice was a challenge at times, but sliding around, once on them, was great fun.

Mike tried to find us grizzly bears, even after touring around grizzly bear countryside, but we never saw one until we arrived in Sitka at a ranger station park, where some had been rescued. He also tried to find us some killer whales, which were normally in the waters in the Inside Passage that time of year, but again Mother Nature kept them hidden. He showed us about everything else he had promised to produce for us. The show was one of the most picturesque ones in our series and one of our most requested to be seen by many.

The coral under the ice was special, too, something I never expected it would look like. Much of it was pure white, like cotton; in fact, most looked like submerged pieces of cotton mixed with a variety of colorful, hard, and soft coral along with green kelp. It was here that we found our first giant Pacific octopus, the largest in the world, hiding in the rock crevices.

It was the second dive location in our series where I used my dry suit, the first being in the Great Lakes with similar temperatures. The dry suit was needed in that cold water for scuba diving, but I can tell you that I sold it upon my return to my home base back in Michigan. While in training when I had first taken the dry suit course years earlier, we had cut a hole in a local lake and gone down through the ice to the bottom of the lake in training. Later, I used it while filming our show *Shipwrecks of the Upper Great Lakes of Michigan*, and now in Alaska, but I decided I had had enough cold-water diving to last me. A dry suit is very stiff, cumbersome, and heavy to wear, but it serves a purpose in keeping us dry, even though we could be down only around fifteen minutes under the ocean in those cold temps before surfacing. When we came up, our hands were so stiff, red, and cold that we couldn't take our own gloves off; we had to have someone else remove them and even assist us in taking off the heavy, zippered suits. Soon I would return to warm water, going from the icebergs back to the underwater volcanoes of Indonesia.

In November 2009 after another DEMA show, I met up with Roman again, the owner of the *Ocean Rover*, in Indonesia. He again invited me to go with him, along with most of the same divers I had been with before on his boat a year prior, in 2008. This time he would take us to the infamous Raja Ampat area for a dive that is on the wish list of most divers today. In this location, marine biologists are discovering new marine life almost daily. Roman had previously talked with all of us from the last trip with him in North Sulawesi, since this next trip was to be a reunion of sorts, getting together with the same group as last year.

Again, it was a long trip, with many stopovers: Japan, Singapore, and other cities along the way in Indonesia. In future years having a home in the Philippines would give me a place to stop off and relax on the way, taking away the stress of long trips. Also the Philippines is a kind of hub in the middle of Asian traveling. From the Philippines, it is just a short hop and inexpensive airfare to most other countries in Asia, like China, Indonesia, Japan, Hong Kong, Singapore, Guam, Palau, Truk Lagoon, Yap Micronesia, and many other places.

When I arrived in Indonesia the second time, we were ready to produce our twenty-sixth show.

Chapter 25

The Headhunters of Papua New Guinea

Show 26: *Raja Ampat, Indonesia* (Filmed in November 2009)

Join us for this special *Dive Travel* adventure as we travel to the opposite side of the planet to Sorong, Indonesia, and dive off the *Ocean Rover* again at Raja Ampat (known as the Four Kings) located west of Papua New Guinea. Widely considered the planet's most biodiverse coral reefs, Indonesia's Raja Ampat Archipelago has over five hundred forty-one species of hard coral. This equates to over seventy percent of the world's hard coral living here, along with half of the known soft corals of the world, far surpassing any other tropical reef system. To date, one thousand three hundred twenty reef fish species have been identified (and still counting). Considering that the benchmark for excellent fish diversity on any given reef is two hundred or more species and that over half of Raja Ampat's reefs support this number, you might begin to grasp the phenomenon that is Raja Ampat. This incredible diversity, known as the "coral triangle," stretches down from the Philippines to Indonesia and across from Jakarta to Papua New Guinea. It is due mainly to Raja Ampat's unparalleled array of marine habitats. From current-swept, reef points to sheltered, black sand Bays to blue-water mangroves, Raja Ampat's dazzling sites will excite even the most jaded scuba enthusiast. More species of fish and coral inhabit this area than any other place on earth. Marine biologists are continually discovering new life in this newly explored region, and for that reason, many of the dive sites are recent discoveries.

When I arrived on the island of Sorong, I arrived a few days early so we could tour and film the area prior to getting on the boat for another ten-day journey. I always tried to film as much topside in the area as possible, for once on the boat, we were water bound for most of the rest of the trip, usually getting back just in time to make our reservations for the trip back home.

The flight was about as long as I had encountered going to Australia, with many hours hopping from airport to airport in various countries. I started out in Grand Rapids, Michigan, arrived in Detroit, then went on to Japan, Philippines, and then Singapore, spending an overnight at the airport. Then I took a flight to Jakarta, Indonesia, where I picked up a Lion Air flight to Sorong, Indonesia, the town where our boat was to be located.

On my last plane ride from Jakarta, Indonesia, to Sorong, the plane was completely packed with mostly native Indonesian travelers who spoke little English. The plane was a Lion Air jet, a regional airline of Indonesia and an older model, which was small and appeared a little shaky taking off and landing. It was many years later that I learned a Lion Jet like the one I had arrived on had crashed in the waters off Indonesia, killing all on board. How sad and scary! The town of Sorong, Indonesia, was small but very quaint and laid back in what appeared to be a small fishing village. A few days after I arrived, we filmed marching bands in a parade for festivities attended by many schools. The timing was perfect, since I was able to show off their culture through colorful school costumes from the various bands marching along with youthful military academy marchers. It was really great to finally get back on the *Ocean Rover* and meet up with the same crew and fellow customers who had been on our last trip together in Manado, North Sulawesi, Indonesia. It was like a big family get-together and a homecoming, which Roman, the ship's owner, had arranged. Seeing everyone again was a fun time. Nighttime was always a special time for the crew and passengers, since one of the crew played a guitar, and the crew would sing folk songs well into the night under the moonlight and stars overhead as the ship was out on the quiet sea. The crew was crazy at times during the day, though, and they were back to their usual antics, like dunking their smallest divemaster of the crew headfirst into a tank of water.

Ocean Rover at Raja Ampat, Indonesia, west of Papua New Guinea

Roman had just as much fun with the crew as they did. Roman, their boss and captain of the vessel, was from Austria, and he had a slightly high-pitched Austrian accent. At first when he spoke, it shocked me to hear him utter his words. The crew used to closely observe me in silence while I interviewed Roman about the area dives in front of the camera, and when Roman wasn't on the deck, they always pretended to be Roman and me.

Observing this one day, I had to laugh when one of the crew held a make-believe microphone and in a deep voice said, "Hi, I am Gary Knapp, and we are here with Roman; Roman, how is the diving here?" Another shipmate in a high-pitched voice said, "Well, the diving is just awesome here today!" to everyone's belly laughs.

Poor Roman was the butt of all jokes, but it was all in fun; you could never underestimate the daily practical jokes they pulled. At the time of this trip, it was Thanksgiving. Their turkey was okay but not a very traditional meal, though the ship's cook tried his best. Most of the usual food was Indonesian. It was also my birthday that week, and the cook had baked me a special cake complete with candles. The crew and customers surprised me with it, and all sang happy birthday to me. A few years after I was there, I received the bad news that Roman had died. This was sad to hear, since he was younger than me. He loved diving; it was his whole life. He had lived a great life on his treasured *Ocean Rover*.

The diversity of the underwater coral and marine life there was phenomenal, from manta rays to every species known to man and many unknown and unidentified as well. I have to say, it was the only place where after a dive we would come up wondering what it was we had just witnessed seeing under the ocean as we discussed it with fellow divers. That had never happened to me before on any dive other than in the Philippines. It was magical adventure diving to the hilt, not knowing what we might see next in the depths. This was where I found my first electric clam. It was always exciting to see something totally new and different that left me in awe. Now I totally understand how it is that marine biologists are discovering new species all the time here.

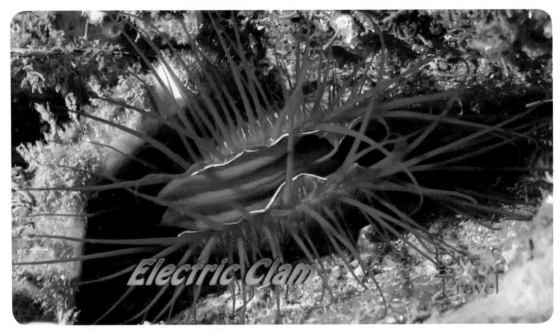

Electric clam, Indonesia

Pink frogfish in Raja Ampat, Indonesia

Raja Ampat diving

We could see some of the land off Papua New Guinea, known as headhunter country from native tribes. We occasionally heard about people disappearing after going through the jungles in years past. It is a very remote part of the world only today occupied by native tribes and described as a "Land of the Unexpected." Recently in the news was the report of a young man who wanted to be dropped off, thinking he could talk to the natives about Christianity only to be killed by a tribal warrior. We certainly weren't going to land there but observing it from a distance from our vessel was always intriguing. We had visited tourist gift shops on various islands that offered interesting wooden Indian artifacts depicting heads and other paraphernalia from the region.

Diving off a rubber dive raft near Papua New Guinea

Finally, in 2009—truly my busiest year of filming ever—I was invited to make a show in Palau, our last show that year. I went to the Philippines, rented a condo for a few days, and took my friend, Sunny, with me this time on a diving trip to Palau. He had never been on a plane before and was so excited that I was taking him with me. He had always longed to go out of the country, but getting visas was a problem for him and other Filipinos at times. But going to Palau wasn't a problem; Filipinos were welcome there. Finally, I would have a traveling companion to help watch my bags for once and a topside assistant and dive buddy to go with me. He would help in running the camera, watching over things to make sure I was framed properly in the stand-up shots I normally did alone, along with interviews. Sunny had previously learned to dive, but he needed more experience. So taking him with me on the short hops from the Philippines to Palau, for example, a couple of hours away, made sense to me. It would be a help to me and give him more underwater time and experience in diving in another country, not that his country wasn't already one of the best to dive in.

Show 27: *Palau* (Filmed in December 2009)

Palau, officially the Republic of Palau, is an island nation in the Pacific Ocean some five hundred miles (eight hundred kilometers) east of the Philippines. Having emerged from United Nations trusteeship (administered by the United States) in 1994, it is one of the world's youngest and smallest nations. Many well-traveled divers place Palau at the top of their list. Surrounded by pristine waters off the western Pacific, the area combines the spirit and culture of the islands with tranquil ambience. On this *Dive Travel* show, we fly into Koror, Palau, and take you on a topside tour of the island's many activities. Our hosts are Fish 'n Fins Dive Center, the Landmark Marina, and the Rose Garden Resort. Being land based, most of our boat rides to nine dive sites are an hour or more away, but Fish 'n Fins also has two liveaboard boats as well. While many of the dive sites are in calm waters, some of Palau's best dives are known for their strong currents and population of large, pelagic animals (those living or occurring in the open sea), such as sharks and rays. Palau is truly a diver's paradise, made up of over two hundred mostly uninhabited islands, with a total human population of only about seventeen thousand. Here we snorkel the famous Jellyfish Lake, or Ongeim'l Tketau, which is one of approximately seventy marine lakes scattered throughout the limestone "Rock Islands" of the southern portion of the main Palau Archipelago. Here thousands of stingless jellyfish surround us like a glove. We also come face-to-face with nine giant mantas on one dive and many sharks and other forms of marine life that inhabit these waters.

Snorkeling in Jellyfish Lake with non-toxic jellies, Palau, Micronesia

This time we were just taking daily trips out on dive boats. On topside tours, we witnessed many hiding holes previously dug into the land and in caves where the Japanese hid in tunnels while fighting Americans during the war. The USA fought Japan back in 1944, and these islands, especially, Palau, Chuuk, and Yap, Micronesia, were the bases for many Japanese troops. The following year, I would be back filming on both Chuuk (Truk Lagoon) and Yap, showing more of their war-torn islands.

Also on the island we toured some awesome, mysterious rock monuments no one seemed to know much about as to their origin. They were much like the mysterious rock formations at Stonehenge. How and when they had arrived there is still a mystery with today's native residents.

Manta ray in Palau, Micronesia

Chapter 26

My First Attack by an Underwater Predator

Show 28: *Aruba* (Filmed in February 2010)

"Bom bini na Aruba" (Welcome to Aruba)!

Aruba is one of the most Americanized islands in the Caribbean. It is always summer here and almost always dry, with an average temperature of eighty-two degrees. Aruba is in the heart of the southern Caribbean, fifteen miles from the South American coastline. The island is just over nineteen and a half miles long and six miles across at its widest point, with a total area of seventy square miles. Unlike the Netherlands Antilles' sister islands, Bonaire and Curaçao, Aruba's topography and vegetation are unusual for a Caribbean island. On the south and west coast are miles of pristine, white, sandy beaches that rank among the most beautiful in the world, rimmed by a calm, blue sea with visibility in some areas to a depth of a hundred feet. The northeast coast, meanwhile, is rugged and wild. The interior is desertlike with a variety of cacti and dramatic rock formations. The island's most famous trees are the Watapana, or Divi Divi trees, all permanently sculpted into graceful southwest bending shapes by the constant trade winds.

Our hosts on this *Dive Travel* adventure are JADS Dive center, The Mill Resort and Suites Aruba, and the Brickell Bay Beach Club & Spa Boutique Hotel. We arrive here to dive the many wrecks found just offshore around the island. Aruba is recently becoming known more for wreck diving, since it has far more wrecks than its sister islands, but the reef's land marine life is spectacular as well.

I was impressed with Aruba; many had said diving wasn't good there, but I found it much like Curaçao and Bonaire. There were more attractions, much more to do topside, and the city was bigger and appeared to be more friendly to American tourists, being somewhat Americanized. But the topography was flat and desert like.

People ask me all the time, "Have you ever been attacked by a shark?" Well, let me tell you of my first and only attack, but It wasn't from a shark. We had been diving and came across this very large, green moray eel lying on the sandy bottom. At first, I thought it was strange that he just lay there out in the open; morays are generally in a reef hole hiding and mostly are shy just poking their heads out. But instead he was in a position where he appeared to be propped up with his head a little higher than the rest of his body with a very bold disposition like "Come get me, you fool."

I started videotaping him to show his size; he was quite long and very large around, fully grown. Another photographer approached him and took pictures when I had finished. The eel just calmly lay there. I waited till the other photographer had finished his shoot, then approached him one last time after the other diver left me alone with him. I wanted to get one more video to show his total length; he had to be at least six feet long. I started with his tail, working my way to his head. When I reached his head, he started to rise off the floor of the ocean, following my camera, which was very large while looming over him. I was doing much like Steve Irwin had done while hanging over the stingray in Australia.

Maybe he saw a reflection in my large glass lens. I don't know, but he kept coming up, at which time I started to rise above him to give him room and try to escape his rise following me. Suddenly, he nailed the right side of my camera lens, striking it hard enough that he pushed me backward. Had the camera not been there, he certainly would have had a piece of me. The response wasn't his fault. In defense of his actions, let me say that most moray eels cannot see very well. They have very limited vision, a blurry vision at best. So he probably thought I was attacking him, and he was simply defending himself. But at any rate, he had my heart pounding for a few minutes after striking my housing, which is made of bulletproof aluminum, and he immediately took off like a shot to the ocean floor below.

When I arrived at the boat above, I told them about the attack, and they were surprised it had happened. Of all my dives and all the marine life I have encountered and filmed around the world this is the only time I was the object of an attack. Never had I thought it would come from an eel, just like I never thought a stingray would attack Steve Irwin. Again, ocean life is unpredictable. I still have a souvenir of his attack with a tooth mark on the outside of the lens, far enough out on the very edge of the lens that it didn't damage the twenty-five hundred dollar super, wide-angle lens on my video housing.

Moray eels can be very dangerous. I have seen videos of a guy's thumb being taken off while he attempted to feed one. I never wanted to get that close to one, for fear of being bitten since they have nasty teeth. I was also told once that when they take hold of you, they don't let go. And their mouths and teeth are full of bacteria, which would certainly infect a person if bitten by one.

One of the many teaching commandments constantly drilled into new divers taking dive courses is to not touch any marine life or coral when diving in our oceans, and for good reason. Not only can we as humans contaminate the coral and marine animals with the oils from our hands if we touch them, but their brushing against us can be even more harmful to divers.

There are several dangerous underwater creatures one needs to stay clear of when diving around the world, especially those that are listed as venomous. Some of the most deadly in Asian and Far-Eastern waters are the Australian box jelly fish that have tentacles covered with biological booby traps known as nematocysts—tiny darts loaded with poison, enough to send one to a watery grave. Many divers can experience paralysis, cardiac arrest, and even death, all within a few minutes of being stung.

The blue-ringed octopuses are quite beautiful to view but are never to be touched. I have witnessed them in the Philippines and Indonesia and photographed several, but they are highly venomous. These creatures can cause nausea, vision loss, loss of motor skills and respiratory arrest. Stonefish, a close relative to the scorpionfish, are pretty common in our oceans but are listed as the world's most venomous fish, along with lionfish known for its many, spiky fin rays, which happen to be highly venomous as well.

Many have heard of the Portuguese man o' war. This sea animal is commonly mistaken for a jelly fish found in large groups floating in warm waters throughout the world's oceans or washed up on beaches. The odds of being killed by one are slim, but this creature can pack a painful punch causing welts on exposed skin. Many larger marine lifeforms such as stingrays can also be dangerous. Most all jelly fish sting but not all are venomous. Sargassum seaweed washed up on beaches can be toxic along with some "blooms" of algae from corals that form in coastal waters, causing red tide which kills fish and makes the surrounding air difficult to breathe.

One time diving off the Florida Keys, in warm ocean waters, I came back home with a red, itching rash, under my diving suit, which appeared to be little red bites. Thankfully, it was the first and only time it happened in my diving career. The itching was so bad, I finally went to see a doctor. He referred to it as sea lice bites, but after some further research, I discovered it was not. Some refer to this as sea lice, but they are not lice at all. They are thimble jellyfish larvae.

Real sea lice are parasites that feed on the blood of salmon and other fish; they do not bite humans. For some reason though, in the 1950s, residents of coastal areas began to call the stings of jellyfish larvae "sea lice bites" and the name just stuck. The jellyfish larvae that cause this condition float in the ocean. When these larvae swim up under your bathing suit, they get stuck and release stinging toxins, which you might even feel pricking your skin at the time of contact. This is the same thing full grown jellyfish do, but it hurts a lot less. The toxins trigger your immune system and cause the bumpy, itchy, red rash, that typically appears four to twenty-four hours after your swim. This condition is like what some people in fresh-water lakes refer to as swimmer's itch. However, swimmer's itch comes from snail beds and duck droppings.

A few of the other smaller marine creatures you may want to observe in the ocean but avoid touching include hydroids, which look like green ocean ferns, also fire coral, certain sponges, sea urchins, the flower urchin, starfish, cone snail, pufferfish, striped pajama squid, and a few sea snakes. Oh my, did I say snakes? Wow! And you thought you were only afraid of sharks in the ocean!

There are many varieties of serpents in the ocean. In fact, the seas are home to more than sixty species of sea snakes that swim and hunt the warm shallow reefs, sea grass beds, corals, and open waters. They are not all poisonous, but some are. It is believed that most of these underwater snakes developed long after their relatives first appeared on land. After all, you have heard of common water snakes or water moccasins in our fresh-water lakes and streams, right? Most fresh-water snakes only swim on the surface but do not live underwater. Most sea snakes living in the oceans are non-aggressive and will only attack a human in self-defense.

I have filmed many sea snakes following them with my camera system as they swam from coral to coral hunting and searching for just the right snack, which is usually made up of small fish. These highly venomous snakes are commonly found hunting on Pacific coral reefs. Many are colorful, but most commonly, I have seen the banded sea snake, all white with black rings encircling its body. Occasionally this snake will rise to the surface of the tropical Pacific to get a gulp of fresh air before descending to continue its hunt. I have filmed a few rising to the surface right over my head only to later sink downward, I had to make certain to be out of its way, I certainly did not want to have it as a neckless around my neck should it fall on me.

I can remember one occasion when I was following a rather large banded sea snake as it ventured around corals looking for food. After all, watching them can be very mesmerizing as their hypnotic bodies meander through the colorful corals. But don't take your eyes off them. I once followed one on camera only realizing later that another one, possibly its mate, was just inches right behind me following me. It was the first time for me to see two or more at once, but it can happen. Sea snakes can range anywhere from three to five feet in length on average, with the largest, the Hydrophis spiralis, getting up to over nine and a half feet in length.

I don't know if this story was true or not, but I was told of a diver once that had a small sea snake sneak inside his wet suit. I can only imagine the sheer terror of that happening. Just be assured, most sea snakes have very small mouth openings, about the size of the tip of your baby finger. The mere small size of its mouth could only be capable of biting a person on an ear or small cartilage area of one's body. Some are bigger, however.

The most venomous sea snake of all is the beaked sea snake (also known as the hooked-nose sea snake), found off the coast of India, Australia, Africa, and the Arabian Sea. This snake is eight times more toxic than a cobra. A mere one and a half milligrams of its venom are enough to kill a human, while a single full dose from one of its fangs can kill about twenty-two people. The only problem is many foreign small exotic islands may not have ready access to the special type of antivenom, also called antivenin, to treat divers suffering from snake bite wounds, especially if they are an hour away from a doctor's office when bitten.

Overall, there are many marine animals as well as corals that can also sting humans. For example, many times you will see schools made up of hundreds of tiny striped eel catfish all swimming together in perfect unison. They look harmless, but even they have spines that are venomous if they touch your skin.

I have filmed most of the creatures listed above at many of the various dive locations I have traveled to around the world, and they appear in many of my hour-long shows. So, yes, there are many creepy, crawling critters, living corals, and plants on our oceans' floors to avoid just as similar plants appear topside in our many forests. Again, a reminder that when God created the oceans below the surface, they are, indeed, like what you see above on land, and both can contain hidden dangers.

Meanwhile, here in Aruba it was the last day of my trip, and it was Carnival weekend. So before I left the island, I spent the day filming their many parades being celebrated on the island. Many dancers were wearing fantastic, colorful costumes as they danced and marched down the streets lined with spectators. Many of the Caribbean Islands host events like Carnival as well. Aruba was a fun place to visit—another party town on yet another exotic island.

At another DEMA show, I found my services were needed once again, this time in the faraway place of Africa. I had made arrangements with the Egyptian Tourism Council with an office located in New York City after meeting a dive shop owner from Egypt that wanted me to spend a full month there touring Egypt and making three shows for the Egyptian Tourism Council. They planned on attending several trade shows around the world, including DEMA, and would be passing out free DVDs of these shows I was to produce for them. The intent was to entice scuba divers around the world to visit the Red Sea and the various dive resorts there, and to show what the world of scuba diving offered divers and tourists coming there. Our projected trip had been in the planning stages for several months while we worked out all the details. I was asked to join them along with Barb, another photojournalist, from Canada, who wrote articles in dive magazines in her home country. I was notified in early 2010 that everything was all set, and they were taking care of all expenses except for my airfare from Michigan to New York's John F. Kennedy International Airport.

This was the first time a dive center and hosting country had offered to pick up the entire tab—roundtrip airfare to Egypt, hotels, meals, and transportation around Egypt by way of boat, car, and more regional airplanes flying to various parts of the country. It took me a while to pack, knowing I was going to be gone almost a month on this shoot and needed everything to film with and produce three shows; that included lots of video tape, chargers, and batteries I had to pack in my suitcases.

Soon I was off to produce shows twenty-nine, thirty, and thirty-one in June 2010.

Chapter 27

Sitting on a Camel in Front of the Pyramids

I left Michigan for New York City, arrived at Kennedy International Airport, and was soon waiting in line for a flight on EgyptAir airlines. Then I was off for my first-time flight into Africa. I hadn't yet thought about the fact that I was really going to Africa.

When I think of Egypt and the Red Sea, Africa doesn't really seem to come to mind. But we were here in Northern Africa and in a country where we would travel through time in a land that had existed before the birth of Christ with a culture rich in history. It appeared to me to be the most foreign soil I would soon tread of all the countries I had visited to date. I was a little worried about safety, since there was also a regional war going on in the nearby Arab countries surrounding Egypt at the time. Steve Rattle, the owner of the dive resort, Pharaoh Dive Club, whom I had met with his wife at a trade show earlier, guaranteed my safety. In fact, they would be hosting Barb (the Canadian photojournalist) and me on this trip around Egypt. They would be our very own personal guides. The language there was Arabic, so it was great having a host translate for us when needed.

I arrived in Cairo, in Northern Egypt, the capital city of Egypt and the most populated city in all Africa. One of the staff members of the Egyptian Tourism Council met me at the airport, and soon I was with Steve and his lovely wife, Clare, and our other photojournalist, Barb, from Canada. I couldn't believe my eyes as we were whisked away to the famous pyramids on camels within mere moments of landing. I sort of had to pinch myself to make me realize this wasn't a dream but was really happening. I hadn't been off the plane more than an hour and a half, not even enough time to take in the surroundings, and here we were, riding on the backs of camels and being guided by a camel caretaker, who was leading us around the world-renowned, great pyramids of Egypt. Talk about being welcomed to a brand-new country!

Watching over the camels at the pyramids

If I was tired, which I was, from the long, exhausting trip, I was suddenly wide awake, trying to hang on to the camel. It isn't easy getting on and off one. Here are some instructions. Approach the hideous beast with caution. Don't let it sense the imminent fear you *will* be experiencing. Do not make eye contact; camels are dangerous and vindictive. If you offend the creature in any way, it will seek revenge. I had to laugh at the funny advice. The camel will get up from its back legs first, so you are instructed to lean back in your saddle as it starts to stand. The camel will then raise its front legs; as it does this, you should lean forward; otherwise you will fall off. They are pretty tall creatures.

My mind vividly raced at the fearful thought and embarrassment of falling off one, since it was a long way down. It is another story all over when they get down to let you off. As they get down, first on their knees, be sure to lean back, since this is where I have seen people fall off, falling forward. If you make it—and you will—it can be a fun and adventurous ride. Their handlers make sure you make it.

When we first arrived at the pyramids, my host talked with personnel at the administration office at the pyramids' front gate. They told him they wouldn't allow me to film with a big professional camera, or they would charge him a small fortune. I guess they thought I was making an expensive movie of some kind, maybe like a big Hollywood film company; my host hadn't thought about that when arranging for me to come. Luckily, I had a smaller video camera along with me that fit in my underwater housing, which I filmed with under the ocean. This one, they thought, looked more like a tourist camera, being small, so they permitted me to use that. I was worried for a while, thinking, *I might not get to film any pyramids,* which would have been a shame since they are the true icons in Egypt.

Filming the Cairo, Egypt show in front of the famous Pyramids of Giza

The three pyramids were an awesome sight; you could see them from far, far away. Just trying to comprehend how they were constructed over a total of twenty years from limestone brought in from the desert was mind boggling enough. The largest, the Great Pyramid of Giza, is one of the Seven Wonders of the World. It is also the oldest of the Seven Wonders of the Ancient World and the only one to remain largely intact. It stands at four hundred eighty-one feet tall and was the tallest man-made structure in the world for more than thirty-eight hundred years until the Lincoln Cathedral was finished in AD 1311. It is estimated that the pyramid weighs approximately six million tons and consists of two and one-third million blocks of limestone and granite, some weighing as much as eighty tons each. There are three known chambers inside the pyramid built to house the burial sites of the great pharaohs of the country.

We also toured the Great Sphinx of Giza, located nearby, which depicts a half-man, half-lion icon built in the third millennium before Christ. We also toured the Grand Egyptian Museum in Cairo in Tahrir Square (also known as Martyr Square), holding over one hundred twenty thousand items. It was, however, just a short time after being there in 2010 (the very next year, in fact), during the Egyptian Revolution of 2011, that the museum was broken into. Two mummies were destroyed along with several artifacts, and some fifty objects were lost. While we were there, it was incredible seeing history come alive all around us.

After filming and seeing all the camels and Egyptian herders of the camels, we wanted to give the herders a tip, but we had been told not to tip the herders, since the owner of the camels would confiscate their money and not give the individual camel caretaker the tip. So I had my caretaker lead me on the camel to a quiet area nearby, and I secretly slipped him the tip so he would indeed be the one to receive it. The camel herders were friendly and hardworking; they certainly deserved a reward for helping us get on and off the camels safely and for walking them around with us on their backs. Soon we were out in the very hot desert to film the opening of our first show with our host, Steve.

Show 29: *Egypt, Cairo, and the Sinai Peninsula* (Filmed in June 2010)

The script on the DVD box cover reads as follows:

> Welcome to Africa. We are here in Egypt to make a series of shows on the Red Sea and the treasures of ancient Egypt. With the fantastic array of both underwater and monumental treasures Egypt has to offer, there was no way to get it all done in one show. In this *Dive Travel* adventure, we are going to visit the main gateway of Cairo, with its iconic pyramids. Then we'll travel into Asia and the Sinai Peninsula to the Red Sea resorts of bustling Sharm El-Sheikh and laid-back Dahab (formerly a Bedouin fishing village). In other shows we visit Luxor and the Eastern Desert region featuring undiscovered diving at the "Jewel of the Red Sea," El Quseir. In another show, we sail off on a liveaboard, *Bella 1*, exploring the myriad of wrecks south of the Gulf of Suez. Helping me on this epic journey as we travel through this amazing country of Egypt is Steve Rattle, who is both my personal host and my tour guide from the Pharaoh Dive Club. We begin our journey with a topside tour of the wonders of modern and ancient Cairo, then dive the beautiful reefs off Sharm El-Sheikh and Dahab. Our sponsor hosts for this show are Afifi El Shimy from Learning Through Travel; Osama Roshdy of Pharaoh Divers; and Sharm El Sheikh and Khaled Amin of Sub Sinai Dive Center in Dahab. Now sit back and enjoy the wonders of ancient Egypt as we take you to Cairo and the Sinai Peninsula.

As you can see, with all the strange Egyptian names, this was going to be a rough show for me to get through in both remembering and introducing all these host of characters, not to mention all the physical Egyptian towns, villages, and seaports we would visit along the way. It seems I was always working my hardest there. On the go all the time, I had to get interviews with all the hosts to give them plugs in the show, since they were the sponsors. I had to constantly haul around my tripod, camera, and sound system to film all the hotels, both inside and out, and prepare scripts to produce a fully blown hotel commercial for each hotel we stayed at. All these hotels were five-star resorts.

I have made my share of commercials over the years, working in both radio and television, but this put me to the ultimate test in producing commercials for these world-class resorts. It is good I had that background in both writing scripts and editing video. We showed everything from the hotels' entryways to the elegant rooms—and not just one room; we showed several types of accommodating rooms being offered. Then on to the restaurants we went, showing their chefs at work in the hot and busy kitchens and the buffet tables with some of the most scrumptious food on the planet.

I had to work lighting and get good angles to show the hotel and its restaurant in the best possible presentation. So each commercial was a work of art. By the time night arrived, I was dead tired only to get up at the crack of dawn and do it all over again. For the next three weeks, the schedule continued; this was more like work than a vacation, and everyone back home thought I was just having the easy life. Oh, I wasn't complaining; it was, after all, an adventure of a lifetime. Who could possibly complain about that? God is good.

At laid-back Dahab, it certainly was that and more. Finally, time to relax. We rested in Bedouin tents in a small village along the seashore. It was so relaxing in the shade of the big tent while being propped up by big, colorful, red pillows piled on the ground in the cool shade away from the hot scorching sun, where we watched camels ride by, carrying equipment on their backs and children also riding them, led by natives of the region. We later rode camels again to experience them carrying us and our dive equipment. They were offering us a preview of what it would be like to take a camel ride along a route to a dive center. The dive shop actually offered several day trips by camel; we didn't have the time to do that, but in the program on Egypt, we show just how they load dive gear on a camel, including air tanks and all the rest of the gear. We rode them once again for the camera in the desert, with the Red Sea in the background. It even appeared like I was getting used to camel riding … not!

When we stopped at roadside areas to rest, we were always greeted by the very young and even some adults selling postcards, souvenirs, picture books of the area, jewelry, and anything and everything that could be sold. I felt the eagerness among all those approaching us to earn some money from us tourists, who were traveling, getting out of buses and cars along the way. I am sure seeing me, an American, brought hope of money, since they all think Americans are rich; and I need to admit that, compared to them, we are.

I have seen how the poor live in our country, including the homeless and those without jobs, but even they, compared to the people I have seen in third-world countries, are far better off. I witnessed some street begging in some foreign countries in past travels—in places like Indonesia and the Philippines—but it wasn't frequent, even though the average wage there at the time was about one hundred forty dollars a month. But here in Egypt, life was far worse. The average wage was eighty dollars per month; some, I was told, were happy to get twenty dollars a month to live on. That's unbelievable!

People here were trying to sell items to save face, but for the most part, most of them were little more than street beggars looking for a handout. I felt so sorry for them, especially when I saw a woman begging for money to buy food for the baby in her arms. She approached us on the street with her fingers to her lips, showing she was hungry and needed milk to feed the baby. Not just one or two but many women and men were all doing the same thing. I passed out some money, but you cannot begin to support everyone you see. Even little kids were begging; I didn't know whether their parents had put them up to it or not, but I was told to watch out since there were many people asking for money. The sights made me feel sad, guilty, and somewhat uncomfortable at the same time, knowing many were desperate and in need.

As a photojournalist, I even discovered that subjects in my pictures also wanted to get paid. That was a first for me. For example, I couldn't take a picture of anyone in Egypt without the person getting off his or her horse, ox-drawn cart, or wagons. The person came with hands out, asking to be paid for his or her picture. I even witnessed an eighty-year-old man abruptly get off his ox-drawn cart to get his coins. This routine later became somewhat funny to me, since my tour guide and host were running behind me, passing out money to all whom I had taken pictures of. I thought, *Well, if I get the poorest people in the pictures, they will each get their just reward.*

Suddenly, I was having fun! But it still made me feel bad that so many in Egypt had to live like this. I always thought in my many travels that I wished I could bring kids from America with me to see places like this. Maybe then for the first time they would begin to understand what it is like to be not only poor but really, really poor and not get everything they want. Here in the USA kids complain when they don't have the latest up-to-date cell phone or other high-tech gadgets being offered. It would be a real learning experience for them to see the other side of the planet. Maybe they would realize how truly blessed they (and we) are to live in the USA.

Show 30: *Egypt, Luxor, and the Eastern Desert Region* (Filmed in June 2010)

Again, the cover script reads as follows:

> Welcome to Africa. We are here in Egypt to make a series of shows on the Red Sea and the treasures of ancient Egypt. With the fantastic array of both underwater and monumental treasures Egypt has to offer, we simply couldn't get it all done in one show. In this *Dive Travel* adventure, we are going to travel south from Cairo to the Eastern Desert region, flying into the coastal resort of Hurghada. Here we will transfer to the road for an additional one hundred miles to one of the Red Sea's best kept secrets, El Quseir, known as "The Jewel of the Red Sea." The coastal road south of El-Quseir runs through some of the most amazing landscapes in Egypt, with a shimmering, turquoise sea; long, empty stretches of beach; and huge expanses of desert disappearing into the distance. That isn't all the region has to offer. When we drive inland to the beautiful Nile River, we discover the awe-inspiring city of Luxor, where we find some incredible ancient monuments, such as Karnak Temple and the Valley of the Kings. On our other Red Sea shows, we visit Cairo in depth, traveling on to the Sinai Peninsula with all it has to offer. Plus we spend a fantastic week on *Bella 1*, taking a Red Sea liveaboard cruise and visiting the awesome wrecks of the northern Red Sea. Here to help me open this epic journey as we travel through Egypt is Steve Rattle, my host and tour guide, of Pharaoh Dive Club. Before we visit Luxor and the Eastern Desert region, we couldn't miss the opportunity to take you on a topside tour of Cairo, our gateway into Egypt. Our hosts for this show include Learning Through Travel, the Pharaoh Dive Club, and Mövenpick Resort in El Quseir. Sit back now and come along with us as we take you on an awe-inspiring journey to Luxor and the Eastern Desert region of Egypt.

These scripts may seem repetitive, and they are, because we were producing three shows, a miniseries from Egypt. All three introductions like the one you just read and the one below were to help promote the three separate DVDs that would be released individually, so each show promoted the others offered in the series.

The Karnak Temple, commonly known as Karnak, comprises a vast mix of decayed temples, chapels, pylons, and other buildings near Luxor in Egypt. The cult temple was dedicated to the gods Amun, Mut, and Khonsu as the largest religious building ever constructed. The Great Temple at the heart of Karnak is so big that St. Peter's, Milan, and Norte Dame Cathedrals would all fit within its walls. Wandering around it was inspiring while trying to think just what it must have been like to see the people there during ancient times just after it was constructed.

Later, at the Valley of the Kings, also known as the Gates of the Kings, is a valley in Egypt where, for a period of nearly five hundred years (from the sixteenth to the eleventh centuries BC), rock-cut tombs were excavated for the pharaohs and powerful nobles of the new kingdom. The valley stands on the West Bank of the Nile, opposite Thebes, modern Luxor. It consists of two valleys—East Valley, where most of the royal tombs are situated, and West Valley. The valleys are known to contain sixty-three tombs and chambers. Some tombs have over one hundred twenty chambers within them.

One thing I noticed in diving all the locations in the Red Sea in all three shows was how very clear, clean, and warm the Red Sea was, like in Asia. The corals were most beautiful and colorful, as was the marine life. Tourists come from all over the world to dive here, and I could see why after diving the pristine reefs.

Show 31: *Egypt, Wrecks of the Northern Red Sea* **(Filmed in June 2010)**

Welcome to Africa. We are in Egypt to make a series of shows on the Red Sea and the treasures of ancient Egypt. On this *Dive Travel* adventure, we fly into Hurghada, where we join the crew of the *Bella 1* for a cruise in the northern Red Sea, diving the awe-inspiring wrecks located in that region. Here divers have an option of extending their stay, adding land-based trips to other regions of the country, such as Sharm El-Sheikh, Dahab, or El Quseir. On this journey, we board the *Bella 1* with other divers from Denmark for an incredible seven-day adventure. In other Red Sea shows, we visit Cairo in depth with a tour of its iconic pyramids and travel into Asia to visit the Sinai Peninsula and what it has to offer, with the bustling Sharm El-Sheikh and laid-back Dahab. Continuing the adventure in further programs, we visit Luxor and the Eastern Desert region, taking in the undiscovered "Jewel of the Red Sea," El Quseir. Before we board the *Bella 1*, we take you on a topside tour of the wonders of modern and ancient Egypt, visiting Cairo, Luxor, and Hurghada. Our sponsors for this *Dive Travel* show are the Pharaoh Dive Club, Seasafaris. net, and the Egyptian Tourist Board. Sit back and enjoy the wonders of ancient Egypt and the wonders located deep within the depths of the ocean as we reveal the magnificent wrecks of the Red Sea in the Gulf of Suez.

Looking out the porthole of a shipwreck in the Red Sea

I enjoyed our underwater tour of many great shipwrecks; the biggest was the *SS Thistlegorm*, a British armed Merchant Navy ship built in 1940, four hundred thirteen feet in length. She was sunk on October 6, 1941. Here we learned how a World War II steamship loaded with supplies for British troops was turned into an undersea time capsule and one of the most-dived wrecks in the world. It was loaded with all kinds of military machinery when it sank during the war by German aircraft. It is often heralded as the most popular wreck in the world; that's not surprising given its well-preserved structure, wealth of World War II artifacts, and its trove of trucks, tanks, and trains now located at the bottom of the sea.

Tractor on a shipwreck in the Red Sea

Scuba diver swimming through the giant propellers of a shipwreck in the Red Sea

Machine gun mounted on a shipwreck in the Red Sea, Egypt

The shipwreck that stood out above all others to me, however, was an Egyptian ferry boat that sank instantly in the middle of the night. The *Salem Express*, a passenger ferry, was returning from Mecca on December 15, 1991, a journey thousands of Egyptian Muslims make every year. The ferry was packed full of pilgrims. The official count says six hundred fifty were on board, of which four hundred seventy perished. However, others claim as many as sixteen hundred may have been on board. If, in fact, that is true, it would make this the worst maritime disaster of all time, even more so than the most famous shipwreck of all time, the *Titanic*.

The *Salem Express* was built in 1976 and was one hundred meters by eighteen meters. A violent storm propelled it into the Hyndman reef, where a hole was ripped in her side. It sank just after midnight, and sadly most of the passengers couldn't swim; it was dark, and there was no one to help with a rescue. It wasn't possible to remove all the bodies from the ship, and it was eventually sealed with all souls inside. She is now a gravesite memorial and a tribute to those who lost their lives.

I was lucky to be taken on the dive; my divemaster, an Egyptian, was reluctant at first, as even I was, due to the sadness of the event. But he offered to take me where most divers never get to go. Diving her can be a very emotional experience and should be undertaken with respect to those who perished. The sad part was due to it sinking in mere minutes; lifeboats weren't even released, since they didn't have time. Yet those intact lifeboats sit lonely and empty today, submerged beside the ship, as if they are still waiting for souls to board them on the floor of the sea.

Eel on a shipwreck in the Red Sea, Egypt

I really enjoyed my tour of Egypt, including my river trip, floating down the Nile River, the longest river in the world. It was way too much to write about here. Even in the three shows that total three hours, we cover a lot of ground, but that was just a very brief synopsis of all the history this country holds so dear. My host wanted me to come back the following year and tour Jordan and other great historic sites and dive locations, making a couple of more shows. Unfortunately, a revolutionary war broke out in Cairo, Egypt, in 2011, a year after I left, and it was unsafe to return.

The Sinai Peninsula is a land of rocky, mountainous desert just off Sharm El-Sheikh, made up of sediment rock in the northern area and granite in the south, surrounded by red-colored sand in all directions extending out into the desert and along the beautiful Red Sea. I thought, *Maybe that is where the Red Sea name comes from.* But, no, it got its name from a type of algae called Trichodesmium erythraeum, which is found in the sea. When these blooms of algae die off, they appear to turn the blue-green color of the sea to reddish brown; thus it is called the Red Sea.

Mount Sinai (seven thousand four hundred ninety-seven feet high), also known as "Moses' Mountain," is known as a collection of peaks referred to as the "holy mountain" and the biblical name for where Moses received the Ten Commandments. It is the land where Moses led the Israelites out of Egypt and across the Red Sea. After forty years of wandering the desert, Moses died on Mount Nebo within sight of the Promised Land.

When I was at Mount Sinai and St. Catherine's Monastery, located nearby, I wanted so much to walk up the mountain. It has three thousand seven hundred fifty steps, hewn out of stone, all the way up the mountain, a long journey. We did see a burning bush by the cathedral, but I wanted to walk up the mountain and see the sight Moses had looked over, but it was a day trip. We were being hosted and had limited to time. I still regret not going up the mountain when I was there and so very close.

People always ask me when I show my films on Egypt whether I saw any wreckage under the Red Sea of horse carriages and Roman gear, where God parted the waters of the Red Sea. The short answer is no; we didn't get a chance to search that area, but I have heard reports of some artifacts being found there. Be it true or not, I have no idea. We did pinpoint, however, about where the Israelites might have crossed—in a northern, narrower finger of the Red Sea. It is a shallower area of the sea, and scholars believe it is the site where waters could have easily parted. The crossing of the Red Sea is part of the biblical narrative of the escape of the Israelites, led by Moses, from the pursuing Egyptians, described in the book of Exodus. Moses holds out his staff, and God parts the Red Sea. The Israelites walk on dry ground and cross the sea, followed by the Egyptian army, which the sea subsequently engulfs.

Kissing turtles in the Red Sea, Egypt

Chapter 28

1944's World War II Operation Hailstone

Later in August 2010, I was invited to one of the premier, historic dive locations in the world, sought after for exclusive wreck diving, along with a second island, called Yap, in Micronesia. I would be about ten days at each location.

Chuuk, Micronesia—or as it is called by the dive industry today, Truk Lagoon—is the site of the United States 1944 bombing of Japan's royal fleet of naval ships, many of which were responsible for the bombing of Pearl Harbor earlier in 1941. It is the site where the United States got even with Japan for the bombing of Pearl Harbor. Some fifty-three vessels lay on the bottom of the lagoon in waters not much deeper than a hundred feet or more, making it a shipwreck-diving capital of the world, so to speak. Divers into shipwrecks come here from all over the world. In fact, mention Truk Lagoon to any would-be wreck diver, and you will find it is on his or her most-wanted wish list of dives.

After a stop at the house in the Philippines and a brief stopover in Guam to get a connecting flight, I arrived in Micronesia to begin another ten-day dive adventure. Again, the box cover gives the details of the show:

Show 32: *Truk Lagoon, Chuuk, Micronesia Shipwrecks* (Filmed in August 2010)

> Welcome to Chuuk, located in the Pacific Ocean in Micronesia, about halfway between Honolulu and Manila, Philippines. Better known by its wartime name of Truk, the lagoon is world renowned for its wreck diving. Chuuk is one of four island states making up the Federated States of Micronesia, which consist of some six hundred tiny islands and atolls stretching almost the entire width of Micronesia, eighteen hundred miles across the Pacific Ocean. Divers come from all over the world, flying into Chuuk International Airport, to arrive at this world-renowned wreck-diving location, which is on the wish list of most wreck divers today. Here you can experience firsthand the underwater museum, graveyard, and the many tombs softened by time and nature into beautiful living reefs. In February 1944, this island was part of Operation Hailstone, in which the United States took its revenge on Japan for the Pearl Harbor bombardment by bombing the Japanese fleet anchored inside Truk Lagoon. Here in Truk Lagoon is the reminder of the World War II disaster and the many Japanese wrecks, which lie close to the islands, such as the *Fujikawa Maru*, *Heian Maru*, and *Shinkoku Maru*. Approximately fifty to sixty other shipwrecks and many planes rest at the bottom of the vast, but mostly shallow, lagoon. Many of these ships are still intact, and some still have human bones and live weapons on board. Today life on this small, tropical, lush island inside the lagoon is laid back and tranquil, but during World War II these islands, being held hostage, were the Japanese Empire's main base in the South Pacific theater. Here we show you Japan's military communication command center, which is now used as a local high school. Our host on this island is the Truk Lagoon Dive center at the Truk Stop Hotel. Join us as we take you back in time to this war-torn tropical island and show you shipwrecks from 1944.

Nippo Maru, 350-foot, five-hold freighter, with two-man Japanese
tank on deck at Truk Lagoon, Chuuk, Micronesia

Collection of ship items outside the *Shinkoku Maru*, a Japanese ship sunk
during Operation Hailstone during World War II at Truk Lagoon

You may have noticed that most Japanese ships have the last name of Maru; the word *maru*, means "circle." The term is used in divination and represents perfection and completeness or the ship as "a small world of its own." The myth of Hakudo Maru is of a celestial being who came to earth and taught humans how to build ships.

This show was very emotional for me while seeing the hundreds of bombs piled on top of one another inside these ships, still preserved under the sea: from long-line torpedoes standing on end all around me inside these dark rooms inside the ships to aerial bombs I saw falling in war films from airplanes above. These ships are still loaded with Jeeps, trucks, military tanks, and weapons of all types. Many of the ships I toured, one hundred feet below the surface, had taken part in the actual Pearl Harbor bombing. Hospital gurneys and medicine bottles littered the floor of some of the ships, along with bones and a sailor's skull melted to the side of one ship's engine room.

Human bones and medical bottles on a gurney on board the *Shinkoku Maru*, a sunken Japanese ship in Truk Lagoon, used in the bombing of Pearl Harbor

Just a few of the many small aerial bombs still on board a sunken Japanese ship, Truk Lagoon, Chuuk, Micronesi

It was very sad to swim through these ships while trying to comprehend the cost of war and lives lost on both sides. While I was diving, a couple of quotes from the late Corrie ten Boom, whom I had met early on, came to mind from her books. She said, "If you look at the world, you'll be distressed. If you look within, you'll be depressed. If you look at God, you'll be at rest." And another quote: "There is no pit so deep that God's love is not deeper still." This site truly represents a horrible and tragic time in our world. I produced this film as a tribute to all those men and women from both countries who had lost their lives there. I would later have another tribute show from Hawaii as a sequel from the site of Pearl Harbor.

I now have to say that of all the shows I produced, this one I especially feel is one of the best I ever brought to fruition. Its aftermath shows a culmination of violence from the past between two countries in a war museum now lying deep below the sea. Seeing the war-torn ships and planes lying on the bottom of the Pacific, many with giant holes blown into their sides and torn apart from the destruction of war, was a sharp contrast to the coral that now, years later, has grown to cover these ships. The beautiful, colorful coral blossoms encasing the ships look like a peaceful casket blanket of flowers over a solemn tomb, which only God could have made, to put them at rest.

Mitsubishi, G4M Navy attack bomber, nicknamed "Betty," World War II, Truk Lagoon

Flowering coral attached to shipwrecks, Truk Lagoon

God's flowering coral, covering a Japanese shipwreck burial ground, Truk Lagoon

Show 33: *Yap, Micronesia* (Filmed in August 2010)

Welcome to paradise, Yap style. Yap, one of over six hundred islands and atolls, is located in the South Pacific, in Micronesia. Here is where the mysterious and legendary stone money, ancient traditions, and the friendliest people in the Pacific lure visitors searching for a memorable vacation. Scuba enthusiasts come from all over the world, since this island is known for magical manta encounters and offers over fifty dive sites just offshore, a short boat ride away. Here we will find exciting sharks, lush walls, macro critter dives, and of course many trips to the manta channels. This island is a wonderful mix of past, present, and future, where an ancient culture exists side by side with the twenty-first century. Located on the Western Caroline Islands, Yap is considered the most traditional corner of Micronesia. It opened for tourism in 1989. Yap offers a unique glimpse into island culture and civilizations far removed from that of foreign administration. On this island, we take a walk through the lush, green jungles and witness scantily dressed native dancers performing for us in this Pacific island paradise. We are also told the ancient story of the mysterious and mostly gigantic circular stones, some standing eight to ten feet tall. They were once used as actual money on this island. Much of it was handmade in Palau and brought over the ocean by small handmade rafts to Yap. People there could buy a house and almost any expensive item with a special wheel made of stone, just as easily as with money. We will also take a land tour and see Japanese planes shot down over the island by Americans during World War II. Our host on Yap is the Manta Ray Bay Resort & Yap Divers. Join us now for this mysterious tropical island tour.

Here we met a native tribe, whose members climbed coconut trees to bring down food for islanders and tourists alike. These natives were scantily dressed but reflected the culture of the island. The women easily wove baskets out of pandanus leaves. First, they boil the leaves, then let them dry in the sun before weaving them into attractive baskets they sell to tourists. The island money used to be huge stone wheels—money used in ancient times by which to purchase goods. While these were made on other islands, natives had to float them across to the island of yap, where they reportedly lost some in the waters off the island during storms while trying to cross with the heavy wheels. The island's jungles show the destruction of wartime, with a former makeshift airport, landing strips, and damaged planes shot down by the Japanese Army. The villages are small and exotic, and the dive shop offers great diving, where we loaded our gear up on dive boats right outside our hotel.

Native dancers performing in Yap, Micronesia

Chapter 29

The Four Main Islands of Hawaii; Bohol, Philippines; and the Sea of Cortez

The next two shows are back in the United States. There, after making the necessary arrangements with the promotions department of the Tourism Council in Hawaii and dive shops on each island, I was set to film the main four tourist islands of Hawaii. First, we did Maui, then the Big Island of Hawaii in part one; and in part two, I was to film the islands of Oahu, and Kauai. My youngest daughter along with her husband, whom I call my son, and their two children as well as part of my six grandchildren decided to go along with me. My daughter and son-in-law had been married in Maui, and they wanted to return there.

We all flew there from California and arrived in Maui at a small cottage the dive shop had arranged for us to stay in. It was my first time on the Hawaiian islands. While the diving was nice, it wasn't on the list as a top dive destination, but topside the place was obviously astounding. The corals were few, and mostly the ocean's bottom was made up of volcanic rock spilled down from the surrounding volcanoes. Lots of marine life was there but few colorful reefs, due to the volcanic activity. We toured the countryside and saw huge fields of pineapple. The landscape is beautiful year-round.

My favorite topside attraction on the Big Island was a helicopter ride over the Kilauea Volcano, on the southeast side of the Big Island. It is one of the most active volcanoes on earth. Major eruptions started in January 1983 and continue to this day. Seeing the hot, boiling lava and fires erupting inside the volcano while looking down from above was breathtaking. Often during the year, a flow of lava can be seen rolling down the side of the mountain and cascading into the ocean below.

Show 34: *Hawaii: Maui and the Big Island, Part One* (Filmed in May 2011)

The box cover reads as follows:

> On this first of a two-part series from Hawaii, we will be visiting two of the four main islands: Maui and the Big Island of Hawaii. We first arrive in Maui and will tour the island's rich countryside, gardens, mountains, beaches, waterfalls, and zip lines. Then we will dive the ocean's depths, where we swim with big sea turtles and pass through historic lava tubes. Our dive host in Maui is Ed Robinson's Diving Adventures, located at Kihei, where we stay at his Koki Hale Deluxe Suite. An additional host is the Aston Maui Lu in Kihei, where we enjoy a native luau, complete with traditional dancers. We do some world-class diving off the south side of Maui while at Ed Robinson's. We are then hosted by Extended Horizon's divers, who take us to the west side of the island for a day of diving off the Lanai area in lava tube caves.

In part 2 of this series, we fly to the Big Island of Hawaii and arrive at Kailua-Kona, hosted by Jack's Diving Locker and witness nineteen mantas in a feeding frenzy over the powerful nightlights on a night dive. The mantas digest the plankton drawn to the lights right over our heads for forty-five minutes of exciting, continuous action. Later, we take both a road trip and a two-hour helicopter tour of the island and journey over miles of plantations, tropical rain forests, hidden waterfalls, and the island's coastline on our way to Hawaii's active Kilauea Volcano. There we see the deep crater with its red-hot lava boiling inside and billowing smoke. "Mahalo" (a Hawaiian welcome)! Now sit back and enjoy this first of our two-part series from Hawaii.

Lava-filled crater at Kilauea Volcano, the Big Island, Hawaii

The Big Island with the volcano had some awesome diving with mantas. The dive shop took us out at night just before dusk and set up bright lights on the ocean floor and lit up the night. It was then that the mantas came in to feed on the plankton while attracted to the bright lights in the ocean. Soon we had nineteen mantas diving and churning up the water all around the lights in a feeding frenzy. Some nights more appeared or less, depending on the night. Later, we were taken out to the deep sea, where it was almost bottomless, and floated on the surface in the moonlight while watching different sea life ascend to the surface. There the organisms glowed and moved in front of us.

This was pretty much the same as when we used to see fireflies on a summer night. The fireflies produced light through a chemical reaction in their glowing abdomens, a process known as bioluminescence. But did you know that the seascapes can also glow and glitter, thanks to the light-producing abilities of many marine organisms? Some fish dangle a lighted lure in front of their mouths to attract prey, while some squid shoot out bioluminescent liquid instead of ink to confuse their predators. Worms and tiny crustaceans also use bioluminescence to attract mates. The animals can control when they light up by regulating their chemistry and brain processes, depending on their immediate needs. Here on the surface of the sea, it was a magical array of lighted objects glowing in the night waters. It was something I hadn't witnessed before.

Show 35: *Hawaii: Oahu and Kauai, Part Two* (Filmed in May 2011)

On this edition of *Dive Travel*, we fly into Honolulu, on Oahu, the capital and most populous city in the state of Hawaii, where we examine its famous land sites, including a downtown sightseeing tour, and the famous Waikiki Beach, with Diamond Head in the background. We later take a diving tour and view the majestic, scenic coastline surrounding the island and also visit infamous Pearl Harbor for a tribute to those who lost their lives in World War II. Our dive hosts, on Oahu, are Pearl Harbor Divers, Honolulu, and The Courtyard by Marriott Hotel in Waikiki Beach. With Pearl Harbor Divers we make some shore dives off the northern coast in swim throughs, seeing a variety of marine life, as well as a boat dive to see the *Sea Tiger* wreck, located near Waikiki Beach in Honolulu. In part two of this series, we fly to Lihue on Kauai, where our hosts include Bubbles Below Scuba Charters and the Hale Kua Bed and Breakfast, located in Lawai, Hawaii, on the island of Kauai.

We leave by dive boat from the southern part of the island off Port Allen. The distance from Kauai Island is seventeen miles. We ventured on for a total of some thirty-three miles west to Niihau Island, Lehman's Crater, and Niihau Arches for an incredible three-tank diving tour, passing a pod of pilot whales on our way. Our land tour includes a complete drive around the outer island, passing beaches along the way and then taking a colorful, internal route into Kauai's "Grand Canyon" with its rugged, rolling interior mountains and canyons. Later we take to the sky in another helicopter for a breathtaking view of the island, since some sites are accessible only by air. Mahalo (welcome)! Sit back and enjoy part two in our thirty-fifth epic show, this one from Hawaii.

Of all the islands, I liked Kauai best, since it was so tranquil, peaceful, quiet, and calm from the rush of the more populated islands. Here we could drive practically all around the island, seldom passing another vehicle. With its vacant, sandy beaches just a stone's throw away, it was truly an island paradise that awaited would-be tourists. Driving in the interior of the island, we passed the Grand Canyon, which looks very similar to the Grand Canyon out west, only smaller, with its high cliffs, mountains, deep canyons and gorges; the exotic canyon would be a hiker's paradise for sure.

I got a chance to go back to see my friends in the Philippines in 2012. After I arrived, Sunny and I took a flight to Bohol and Palawan Islands, where again I had hosts lined up to offer us diving and a hotel.

Sunny, my Philippine dive buddy and friend, on one of our diving trips

Show 36: *Bohol and Palawan Islands, Philippines* **(Filmed in 2012)**

The Philippines new logo theme "It's more fun in the Philippines" lives up to its name as we return to the Philippines and fly from Manila to the tenth-largest island, Bohol, in the Philippine Sea, arriving at its capital, Tagbilaran City. Our hosts are Philippine Fun Divers and the Lost Horizon Dive Resort, located on Alona Beach, Tawala, Panglao Island, Bohol, Philippines. Panglao Island is connected by two bridges from the mainland. This area is listed as one of the top-ten best diving locations of the world for its pristine beaches, clear water, colorful coral, and abundant and rich marine life. Topside we tour the famous Chocolate Hills, where as many as one thousand seven hundred seventy-six numerous mounds of limestone formations exist. We travel through a mahogany, man-made forest, take a walk across the double-hanging bridge, sample a fresh coconut, take a dinner cruise down the Loboc River, and meet the Ati tribe. Later we look for the elusive Philippine tarsier, considered the smallest primate in the world and indigenous to the island of Bohol. The tarsier is found not only here but also in Indonesia and Borneo. It has been estimated that there are only between five thousand and ten thousand Philippine tarsiers left in the whole world, and that number is believed to be falling. They are very lovable animals but don't live long in captivity. "The world's smallest monkey" is an often-heard slogan; however, it isn't a monkey. In truth, its classification is somewhat problematic. Some scientists consider tarsiers to be a taxonomic suborder among the primates, while others, because they are closely related to lemurs, lorises, and bush babies, classify them with the prosimians to which these animals belong. They live in the trees in dense forests, living on a diet of insects, and have a shy, nervous nature. There are eighteen different species of tarsiers, all primates. This Philippine tarsier is only four and six tenths inches tall, while other species can get up to twelve to fifteen inches. The tarsier are nocturnal hunters, and their large, bulging eyes help them maximize their available light to catch their food and similarly to keep them aware of their predators, like snakes, cats, and monitor lizards.

In the last part of the show, we fly to Palawan Island, arriving in the capital city of Puerto Princesa City, the largest province in the country, which is four hundred fifty kilometers or two hundred eighty-one miles long. The Island of Palawan stretches from Mindoro in the northeast to Borneo in the southwest. It lies between the southwest Philippine Sea and the Sulu Sea. Here we make a few dives off Puerto Princesa City with Moana Dive Shop and explore the topside, consisting of beautiful, white, sandy beaches; take a boat ride inside a famous underground river; fly over the forest on a canopy zip line tour through the jungles; and tour a crocodile nature center.

A Philippine tarsier, the smallest primate in the world

Bohol Island, Philippines, was a spectacular dive region. I fell in love with the marine life and corals there. Nothing exuberates cuteness under the ocean more than a clown fish or what you may know as the real "Nemo." I found clown fish in a variety of colors in both the Red Sea and here in the Philippines. They come in yellow, light orange, orange, and tomato red; and I have even seen light, tan-colored clown fish. Clown anemonefish, with a bright-orange color and three distinctive white bars, are the most recognizable of all reef dwellers. They reach about four and three tenths inches long and are named for the multicolored sea anemone, in which they make their homes.

Anemone fish or clown fish, Bohol Island, Philippines

Tomato clown fish, Bohol, Philippines

These fish simply put a smile on my face whenever I saw them. They looked at me and the camera and appeared to perform before our eyes. Clown fish, known as anemonefish, performed an elaborate dance with the anemone before taking up residence, gently touching its tentacles with different parts of their bodies until they were acclimated to their host. A layer of mucus on the clown fish's skin made it immune to the fish-eating anemone's lethal sting. In exchange for safety from the predators and food scraps, the clown fish drives off intruders and preens its host, removing parasites. There are at least thirty known species of clown fish, most of which live in shallow waters of the Indian Ocean, the Red Sea, and the western Pacific. They aren't found in the Caribbean, Mediterranean, or Atlantic Ocean. Surprisingly, all clown fish are born male. They can switch their sex but do so only to become the dominant female of the group. The change is irreversible.

Clown fish, Bohol, Philippines

Healthy reef with colorful fish in the Philippines

The last show we produced, show thirty-seven, was a trip back to Mexico, where I had a liveaboard dive boat lined up to host me. At the time, I didn't know it would be my last show, but it became so.

Show 37: *The Sea of Cortez, Mexico* (Filmed 2012)

We fly into Phoenix, Arizona, and take a van across Mexico on a four-hour road trip south across the Mexican border to Rocky Point, Mexico (Puerto Peñasco) on the Sea of Cortez, and the Midriff Islands to begin this exciting seven-day dive adventure. This body of water separates the Baja California Peninsula from the Mexican mainland. It is bordered by the states of Baja California, Baja California Sur, Sonora, and Sinaloa with a coastline of approximately four thousand kilometers (or twenty-five hundred miles). Our hosts are Dora and Francisco (Lolo) Sandoval, owners of the luxurious one-hundred-ten-foot-long *Rocio Del Mar* liveaboard, based out of Rocky Point, Mexico. It is the only liveaboard based on the Sea of Cortez. The Sea of Cortez season is from the end of June until the end of October every year. It is here that we snorkel with whale sharks in the emerald waters of the coast, dive with sea lions, and view the largest pods of dolphins I ever encountered, churning up the ocean surface. The Sea of Cortez is surprisingly full of all types of marine life, far more than I ever anticipated.

Here we dive on untouched walls and in reefs abounding with sea life. With clear, deep-blue waters, abundant sea life, white-sand beaches and inspiring vistas, the Sea of Cortez—known as the Gulf of California—is a breathtaking destination for exploring diverse marine creatures. Legendary diver Jacques Cousteau described the Sea of Cortez as the "World's Aquarium" and the "Galapagos of North America." Dive untouched walls and reefs abounding in marine life. Encounter great and small whale species, whale sharks, mantas, and jumping mobula rays (or flying rays), humpback whales, and sea lion colonies as well as sperm whales. Hike and explore remote uninhabited islets in this picturesque sea.

Of the many shows I made around the globe, this was an exciting adventure and closer to home than many places I have been. This sea was overflowing with marine life promised only at other locations. It had a great assortment of large fish, from the whale shark, the largest fish in the ocean, to an abundant supply of seals, to the largest pods of dolphins seen anywhere at one time as they churned the ocean's surface. They leaped out of the water in a vista as far as the eye could see in all directions from the boat we were on while following them. It was truly a magical experience to witness. The Sea of Cortez offers almost everything we would find in any of the many oceans of the world. The sea was mostly calm and clear, and always sunny, warm conditions exist. The liveaboard was the best access to these dive sites. It is a perfect dive site close to home for people in the United States. I would highly suggest it as an alternative to diving the Caribbean.

Dive group just leaving for a dive in the Sea of Cortez, Mexico

Seals frolicking under the Sea of Cortez

A feeding whale shark, which can weigh up to twenty tons, with its mouth open, eating plankton

Whale sharks—the largest fish in the sea, up to sixty feet long—in the sea of Cortez, Mexico

Chapter 30

Coral Reefs, Fish-Cleaning Stations, and Earth's Constant Changes

Coral reefs function like a tropical forest of the ocean or an ocean oasis. Any diver can tell you that coral reefs are beautiful. They are like undersea cities filled with colorful fish, intricate formations, and wondrous sea creatures. The importance of coral reefs, however, extends far beyond the pleasures they bring to those who explore them. Coral reefs play an essential role in everything from water filtration and fish reproduction, to shoreline protection and erosion prevention. Coral reefs provide food and shelter for sea creatures. Coral reefs are spread out over the shallow seas of the world's tropical and subtropical regions.

About one quarter of the five hundred thousand animal species living in the world's oceans inhabit areas with coral reefs. Even some of the fish species living in the outer seas use reefs as places to spawn and raise their fry. Larval fish live off a yolk sac attached to their bodies. When the yolk sac is fully absorbed, the young fish are called fry.

Coral reefs are important for many different reasons aside from supposedly containing the most diverse ecosystems on the planet. They protect coastlines from the damaging effects of wave action and tropical storms, and they provide habitats and shelter for marine organisms. They are a source of nitrogen and other essential nutrients for marine food chains, and they help with carbon and nitrogen fixing and recycling.

Reefs, some of the most biodiverse systems on the planet, are home to roughly a quarter of all marine species. Some six million fishermen around the world derive livelihoods from the reefs, particularly in the developing world. Reef systems help shield coastal communities from the brunt of tropical storms and serve as economic bodies for tourist-dependent communities. But the reefs are in trouble. One of earth's more ancient complex life forms, coral, has proved to be very vulnerable to the higher ocean temperatures and increased acidification brought on by climate change. Mass bleaching events along with disease and the increased frequency and ferocity of tropical storms have decimated reef systems.

The Caribbean alone has lost up to eighty percent of its coral reef cover in recent decades. In Belize, for example, reefs were being rapidly degraded by both changing environmental factors and human development. Particularly damaging is the depletion of the nation's mangrove forest, which has a vital symbiotic relationship with coral reefs; the government stepped in and made changes. Coral reefs can be saved through reseeding and replanting from greenhouse stock, and over time they can be restored, as was the case in Belize. Reefs act as buffers against shorelines, waves, storms, and floods, helping to prevent loss of life, property damage, and erosion.

Healthy coral reefs support commercial fishermen, jobs, and businesses through tourism and recreation. Approximately half of all federally managed fisheries depend on coral reefs and related habitats for a portion of their life cycles. The

National Marine Fisheries Services estimates the commercial value of U.S. fisheries from coral reefs to be well over one hundred million dollars. Local economies also receive billions of dollars from visitors to reefs through diving tours, recreational fishing, trips, hotels, restaurants, and other businesses based near reef ecosystems.

Another problem with coral reefs today is coral bleaching, or dead reefs, as in the case of Australia at the Great Barrier Reef. Coral bleaching, fishing, mining, and the burning of fossil fuels have all contributed to the destruction of the reefs over several decades. For example, ninety-three percent of the Great Barrier Reef off Australia is affected by bleaching, putting the reef in danger of extinction. Bleaching occurs when corals are put under extreme stress by changes in conditions like temperature, light, or nutrients. In these conditions they expel symbiotic algae from their tissues, causing them to turn white, in what is known as coral bleaching.

On a more positive note, one of the things on reefs I have most enjoyed learning is what is known, or little known to the average non-diver, as fish-cleaning stations, and almost every reef system contains them. I always enjoy calling kids up front at lectures to tell them this story, showing pictures about these special stations located in the ocean, which act as doctors' offices. You see, animals such as sponges act like filtering agents in the ocean to help filter the water and keep it clean, since fish can get sick, too, just like people do. I don't mean sore throats or earaches, but they can get bacteria and parasites on their bodies that cause sores and infections.

Fish-cleaning stations are usually located on a reef where a section of it is flat and where no reef obstacles interfere, with the largest patients coming in for a cleaning. And come in they do! Fish-cleaning stations on reefs are like doctors' offices, where certain species like wrasses and gobies in a variety of bright colors live. These doctors don't wear white drab coats like our human doctors we go to, but they instead do a dance while coming in to visit you. These small, colorful doctors dance around on the reef up and down and swim in circles while trying to attract their patients' attention to let them know the doctor is in and ready to treat the patient. Now these much larger patients begin to arrive for checkups and cleaning. Patients of all sizes—from sharks, stingrays, manta rays, groupers, and even bigger fishes like whale sharks—come in for their cleaning.

Sometimes the patients, too, act strange, hanging upside down or going vertical to signal the doctor that they need an inspection. The gobies and wrasses go to work, immediately picking off parasites and infected skin on the fish, totally cleaning them of their wounds. The doctors, you see, get a tasty treat, and the patients get clean. It is a win-win for both the patients and the doctors. Some even act like dentists. Patients such as a shark open their mouths wide while the smaller cleaning fish swim in and out of their mouths, cleaning the inside of their mouths and their teeth, picking off bacteria and left-over food particles, giving their teeth a real cleaning.

Patients, however, need to be very careful not to eat their dentist, since they keep coming back to the reef for more visits. But there is always a bad fish in every bunch who takes advantage of the situation and pretends to be a doctor who really is not. Blennies are sometimes bad fish; they often fake being a cleaner, and when the patient least expects it, they take a bite out of the patient's flesh—and ouch! There is never a dull moment while watching fish at these fish-cleaning stations. Sometimes, if you hold your hand out slowly and calmly, the doctors will even come over to examine you.

Our planet earth is always changing; from volcanoes to earthquakes, time marches on. The ice age had a dramatic effect on the planet, which is still changing today, with ice sheets still left over from its existence. An ice age is a period of long-term reduction in the temperature of the earth's surface and atmosphere, resulting in the presence or expansion of continental and polar ice sheets and alpine glaciers.

But now the earth is warming at an alarming rate in this past decade. In traveling around the world over a period of twelve years, I noticed its effect on the reefs at various places of the world, with the vast warming. In Australia, for example, the Great Barrier Reef, the largest reef system in the world, is mostly dead now. I have seen what warm temps can do to reefs in various parts of the world. I know there are a lot of people out there who maintain we are in only a normal cycle. But if you pay attention to the world, with the melting of the glaciers in the arctic circle and the effects on how the oceans may rise in the next century, you will begin to see more proof of its existence. You only need to go to Genesis in the Bible to look at what happened with Noah's ark when God flooded the earth at that time by having it rain for forty days and forty nights. The result was a great flood. Just look at a recent hurricane, which moved over Houston, Texas, a few years ago. In only a three-day period, the area was flooded with over seventy inches of rain. Can you imagine, had it continued for forty days, what might have happened? Look at where the original shoreline of North Carolina was thousands of years ago. It was forty miles out in the open ocean, where I found the teeth of the megalodon shark I wrote about earlier.

You see, earth will never stand still; it is always on the move, and changes happen over hundreds of years, so, generations don't always see the immediate changes in one's lifetime, but they definitely do take place. Scientists now say it's just a matter of time till the oceans increase their water levels by a prediction of as much as three feet if the ice continues to melt in the Arctic, and it could be up to five feet in the next century, they predict.

Do you have any idea what that prediction means to the world's surface if that were to happen? For every inch of sea level rise, you will see one hundred inches of runup inland on the coast. So, for example, a three-foot rise in sea level would equal thirty-six hundred inches or as much as three hundred feet inland. Can you imagine what would happen to all the buildings around the world located on ocean fronts that would suddenly find themselves within three hundred feet of the ocean and then be surrounded by water? Today, seventy-one percent of the earth's surface is already covered by water, with twenty-nine percent of land mass left. If the oceans increase by an additional three feet, they will be disastrous for many of the low-lying islands and beaches around the world.

What happens if the ice melts in polar regions? About two and two-tenths percent is frozen water. Therefore, our current land mass would drop to nearly twenty-seven percent, and rising seas would increase the oceans to over seventy-three percent. About ninety-seven percent of all water is ocean water; three percent is made up of frozen waters, rivers, and lakes. The effect on the world would show an immediate decrease in inhabitable land as water rise takes over. Shorelands on the mainland areas and low-lying islands around the world would simply disappear under the ocean—and not for a few days, like hurricanes often do with flooding for a short period, but permanently!

This would have lasting effects on parts of Florida, for example, that are only one foot above sea level as it is. They could virtually find themselves underwater with no mountains to go to. Parts of California would be affected along with even New York City, and low-lying islands everywhere around the world could soon be underwater. When I am diving, I see islands under the ocean that at one time were above the surface of the ocean; look at the story of the lost city of Atlantis.

Two areas of the world have always intrigued me: the Bermuda Triangle, located between Miami, Bermuda, and Puerto Rico; and the Dragon's Triangle, located in the Devil's Sea just south of Japan. I have been near each of these areas in my dive travels. Each is on the opposite side of the world from the other, and both are directly horizontal from each other. If you look on a world map, you can draw a horizontal line between them. These areas are the strongest and most polarized regions on the planet, and some people have theorized over the years that these locations have caused planes and boats to go missing. They are some of the mysteries of our planet that offer no real explanation.

Many books have been written about these triangles. For a good read sometime, look them up at the local library and read about all the mysterious disappearances that have occurred; many are still on the current US Air Force and Navy's files of the unexplained. Today planes and ships tend to stay clear of these areas of the world.

Chapter 31

The End of the *Dive Travel* Series

I abruptly stopped producing the series after my show number thirty-seven.

I was supposed to be retired, but it seemed now like the series had become more like a business than a hobby for me. It was becoming more work. While many of the destinations were beginning to support me—taking care of things on their end—back at home, it was my job to continue to uphold my responsibility of working and producing the show to fulfill my responsibility to the hosts. I was also somewhat at their mercy, for I would send the finished product off to have them review it only to have them want more and more changes.

The series finally became too much work, and frankly I got burned out, mainly in the editing process. I had so wanted to produce the top-fifty dive destinations of the world, but it appeared I would have to live with the top thirty-seven and call it quits. I totally enjoyed the filming part while at the destinations; it was a ball. But not coming home with all the footage and having to start all over with producing another show and sifting through thirty-three average hours filmed at each destination. Trimming and editing it down to sixty minutes got old.

I feel blessed beyond belief that God had helped me to accomplish all I did in making the series. I was, after all, pretty much a one-man band. Seeing my shows, people often asked how many helped me, or they asked about the size of my crew. When I told them it was just me out there in the world, traveling and videotaping, they were shocked and seemed in disbelief to hear I had traveled and filmed them all alone, shooting and editing every last inch of video you see in the films. I was surprised at first when people said, "You did all that?" I guess I never really thought much about it at the time, since it was a fun time and very rewarding for me, and I worked on it with great passion, as if it were a regular job, even though I never got a paycheck. I had a few young guys over the years with experience in video editing who helped me part-time on the final edits of the shows; they also assisted me by finalizing and rendering the shows to get them ready for burning on regular DVD and Blu-ray disc. I couldn't have done the job without their final expertise. But they also had other jobs of their own, and it became harder and harder to get them to schedule time to come in and help me make the finishing touches to the products.

I finally sold the *Dive Travel* series in 2016 to Reto Lingenhag, who owns Education 2000 in Fort Lauderdale, Florida; he still distributes the series today. He used to stock all my shows for resale early on, so he was familiar with my product. Both regular and Blu-ray DVDs can still be outright purchased from their company at www.DVDwholesale.net. Just select (Travel) under the list of available DVDs on the left-side column of their screen, and you should be able to scroll through all thirty-seven shows they have on file that we produced. Each individual show has a beautiful color cover we designed for each travel location, which accompanies the DVD. You can enlarge and see them on their website. Scroll through all of them, and you can then see what I described in this book about each location.

If any of the destinations I filmed interest you, you can obtain a regular DVD or Blu-ray disc copy from Education 2000 at www.DVDwholesale.net. See their attached logo below.

Website: www.DVDwholesale.net
E-mail: reto@education2000i.com
Operated by Education 2000 Inc.

On Facebook, people can also still see my two free promos online by liking *Dive Travel* DVDs on our Facebook post. Be sure to hit like on the post to follow us. We give news updates from time to time about upcoming film showings and locations. To keep active, over the past few years I have been showing and presenting my films at churches and lecture halls in both Michigan and Florida, giving talks and sharing information about our oceans, marine life, coral reefs, sharks and their importance in our ecosystem, and the environment. I have shared information over the years with colleges, high schools, and elementary schools. To do this I have a large, portable twelve-foot movie screen, a high-definition projector, and a complete sound system, which I can transport to any event to present my shows. I can even show my films on large, theater-size screens in auditoriums for nonprofit organizations wishing to raise money for any special event they might have.

At these showings, I always get asked lots of these questions:

Aren't you afraid of diving with sharks? Have you ever had any close encounters? How deep do you dive? What is the best location to dive? What is your favorite place?

I get questions about all the marine life and reefs and so on. I get lots of questions, and I am always excited to see the enthusiasm people exhibit and what they want to learn and know more about from our oceans and the marine life inhabiting the deep and not-so-deep waters. I am not a scientific expert, but I have learned from the best marine biologists around the globe, gaining a free college degree of information along the way. These guys are into tagging marine life, cataloguing it, and keeping track of their movements and habitat. They study the oceans and the marine life in great detail and have a vast knowledge of the health of the marine life and corals. It is interesting, too, the questions I get coming from all age-groups and sexes. Men seem to be more interested in shipwrecks, women are fascinated by beautiful coral reefs and marine life, while teens and younger ones love to have me talk about sharks or dolphins. One thing nice about the DVD lineup is that there is something for everyone in each video. In my presentations, I can design a program to fit any age-group.

To answer a few of these questions, no, I am not afraid of diving with sharks. My diving has taken me down in the vast oceans with thousands of sharks, and not once has one ever been aggressive toward me. I have been on many shark feeds, with many sharks feeding in a frenzy and circling around me. In my talks about sharks, I sometimes equate some sharks' aggressiveness to that of farm animals like bulls, since I had experience in working with bulls on the small dairy farm where I grew up as a teenager in Michigan. For the most part, bulls won't bother you, but on rare occasions, one will turn on you, as it did on me once.

A bull from our small, rural farm in southern Michigan had gotten out of our pasture one year and into a herd of cattle at our neighbor's place. So now our young bull was king for a day, overseeing the new herd of cows, and he wanted to show he was the bull of the herd. Well, I went in after this farm animal that in the past I could easily approach, but this time he seemed different. I guess his testosterone was at an all-time high. When I went after him, he simply put his head down and looked at me with those steel eyes, glaring me down. Suddenly, he lunged at me, and all I could do was turn and get out of his way, jumping over an electric fence I didn't even know existed till after I had jumped it. My dad finally had to work hard to get him into a corral.

When I tell this story, I try to show that sharks are like this as well. While most sharks aren't interested in a swimmer or scuba diver underwater, you just might someday come across one that is. That is one that woke up with a bad disposition like that farm bull, one that's hungry and ready for action, one that's not willing to have a diver get in its way in its home beneath the sea, and one that just might chase you out of the water. This story reminds me of a couple of divers who told me a story once about a hammerhead shark that did just that to them in a dive on a wreck off the Florida panhandle. The hammerhead was alone, and he owned the sea and wasn't interested in sharing that region with the divers. He chased them around the wreck and later up to their dive boat and out of the water.

You see, when I filmed a school of scalloped hammerhead sharks off Cocos Island, an island owned by Costa Rica, the sharks there were very timid and acted just the opposite. It was mating season; you would think they would have been aggressive, but they were so afraid of scuba divers' bubbles that unless you practically stopped breathing, which one cannot do underwater, it would have been difficult to even get close enough to a hammerhead to get a picture of it up close. None were violent, and there were no worries. But I was told, find one alone with a bad disposition, as was the case with the two divers I just described, and you could find trouble sometimes, although it has never happened to me to this day. Most sharks are skittish and gentle, and they avoid divers altogether.

As far as close encounters go, the only close encounter I ever had from any living marine species was from a green moray eel off the coast of Aruba, which I told you about. Had I not been holding my camera housing he would have attacked me. I have always had the greatest respect for all marine life in the sea; after all, they aren't in *my* working environment; *I* am the one trespassing in *theirs*.

I think sometimes we individuals get desensitized to fear as we grow older. This truth reminds me of a recent experience. I live on a small, rural lake in northern Michigan. I walk around the two-mile lake once, sometimes twice a day. While walking around the lake one evening before dusk, I noticed a very large, tall, black dog way down the road and heading my way on the same side of the road where I was walking. Running loose and off its leash, as it was, I suddenly became fearful that it might be mean. As I got closer to it, and it to me, I realized when it turned to go down in the ditch after spotting me, that it wasn't a dog at all. Instead, to my amazement, it was a medium-sized black bear!

I was so excited to see my first black bear at home. I was no longer afraid but instead was filled with excitement. I had lived here all these years and heard about bears being around but had never seen one in person, especially in this close encounter on my walking path in the wild. By the time I passed where I had seen him disappear into a swamp, I was disappointed that he was gone. Once I got home, I realized that at first I was afraid of a dog, yet when I saw it was a bear, I was no longer afraid. Instead I was excited. I think this story describes our natural instinct or reaction to adventure.

Fellow divers used to sometimes wonder whether I was like the horse whisperer underwater; they thought I seemed to have a mindset that could understand and read the minds of certain marine life or have a telepathic tune-in with them. I had to admit that many times marine life creatures approached me out of the blue. Maybe God sent them to me so I could film them in their glory; I do believe that has really happened at times.

Once I can remember being in the ocean, off the Bahamas, when two fairly large fish, almost identical in size—and fish I had never seen anything quite like before—approached me. I was alone at the time. I Just remember them being very large, each maybe half the size of myself with exceptionally large, friendly-looking eyes. They took their time looking me over as they swam circles around me for maybe ten to fifteen minutes, constantly eying my every move and me theirs. I imagine they were wondering what kind of creature I was as well, just as I was curious about them. I looked directly into the eyes of these two large fish, and they eyed me as well, never taking their eyes off me for a second. It felt like I could kind of understand their sense of wanting to be there, as strange as that sounds. I was mesmerized and captivated by them and their keen interests in me. I suddenly felt at peace, sharing that special moment in time with them.

It is hard to explain what was happening, and I have to say, I was even disappointed to see them later swim away, leaving me alone. I laughed somewhat after that experience, thinking, *Maybe I am turning into a fish.* I have had many such experiences like this with marine life over the years, with dolphins and so forth. I learned early on to just go down to the bottom of the ocean near the reef and just sit and wait for the various species of fish to approach me. They eventually came to me, unlike my trying to chase them down. This allowed me a closeup view of them instead of my trying to hurriedly follow them, which rarely works for a videographer. The faster I swam toward them, the faster they retreated ahead of me. I had tried that tactic early on over the years, trying to catch up with fast-moving fish, but I found a better technique in just relaxing and being patient.

I often wonder what these marine life species must think of us humans when seeing us for the first time. They must look at us with our heavy scuba tanks on our backs, appearing like a hump, with two long arms hanging down and two long legs with big fins on our feet, appearing as a four-legged octopus. Our eyes are made even larger with our big masks on with eyes peering out and those outrageous bubbles coming out of our heads, appearing like a kind of scary monster from the depths of the sea.

Chapter 32

Scuba Statistics and Best Places to Dive

Today I have a world map, mounted on a pegboard, that is covered with push pins and dive flags pinpointing all the areas around the world I traveled to as well as all those destinations where I dived and filmed. You see, I didn't just go around the world on a one-time trip, but instead I traveled extensively around the world multiple times each year over a twelve-year period. Sometimes it truly amazes me when I look at the world map and see just how far God led me to see His mighty handiworks firsthand. After all, it is His work alone and all that He created. Indeed, I am so blessed, and we all should feel blessed after seeing His mighty, genius works He created that surround us.

How many people scuba dive today? According to the latest statistics, there are between two point seven and three point five million active scuba divers in the United States with as many as six million scuba divers worldwide. Compare that to about eleven million snorkelers in the United States or twenty million worldwide. These numbers, of course, are estimates, and "active divers" means those who dive at least five times a year. Figures also say about five hundred thousand new divers are certified each year. Either way, the numbers are small in comparison to other sports out there, since worldwide only slightly more than one percent of the world's population participates in scuba diving. Of that figure, about one hundred divers die each year in North America, and another one hundred die each year while diving in the rest of the world. According to DAN (Diver Alert Network), most divers die from inexperience as the biggest factor. While you might think these numbers are high, they aren't when compared to other sports; scuba diving is still considered a low-risk activity compared to many other outdoor sporting activities. There are five best scuba diving certificate programs that certify scuba divers. PADI (The Professional Association of Diving Instructors) is one of the best and the largest. The runner-up is SSI (Scuba Schools International), followed by the oldest agency, NAUI (the National Association of Underwater Instructors), and then the British contingent, BSAC (British Sub-Aqua Club); and the best for future technical divers is SDI (Scuba Diving International).

From claustrophobia to a fear of sharks, people give a lot of reasons why they won't get scuba certified. Here are some other reasons: many don't have scuba gear, divers say travel is too expensive, people have problems clearing their ears, and they are afraid of sharks. One of the biggest problems divers tell me about is ear clearing; that alone can end the sport for many. Many people suffer from sinus problems, and then they dive. It is never recommended to dive if there is any pain in the sinus areas, including your ears, eyes, and nose. If you suffer from ear pain during a dive, slowly ascend a few feet until the pain subsides. Once the pressure equalizes, slowly descend at your own pace. If any pain doesn't dissipate, make your controlled ascent and sit out the next dive; then try it again later or even the next day. If this still gives you problems, see a medical professional.

I feel sorry for those who suffer from this condition. I have seen a few sit out their dives while on vacation. Of course, it is sad when one travels to the other side of the planet, only to be disappointed upon arrival with an unexpected cold or sinus problem and have to sit out the dives, but it happens. I remember a lady once on a shark dive boat with me, who told me she and her husband had booked the trip of a lifetime to dive in cages to view sharks, but just prior to the trip, she learned she was pregnant and had to sit out the dives for that reason as well, only allowing her husband to dive. Sometimes illness or unexpected circumstances arise that prevent one to dive. I even had to do it once or twice while having a bad cold. Some just end up permanently ending the sport for this reason altogether.

As for being afraid of sharks, I just shake my head. Many ladies have told me that they won't even go to the beach and stick their toes in the water for fear that a shark might attack them. Many people think sharks are swimming in the ocean and just waiting to chomp into their next victim. And thanks to movies such as *Jaws*, Hollywood doesn't always help. In most cases, sharks want nothing to do with divers. When they notice divers in the area, they typically swim in the other direction. But for real divers, the issue isn't about hoping we don't see a shark. It's instead getting lucky if we do.

Where is the best dive location in the world? I used to say, "My next dive!" (tongue in cheek). The reality is, all of my dive locations have been extra special, just as I have pointed out; each location, both topside and deep under the ocean, offers a unique perspective only from that specific location or region of the world. The answer really comes down to this: just what is it you want to see? What are you interested in? For example, if you want to see great white sharks, it is heading to Guadalupe Island, Mexico; if you want to see giant mantas, it is going off the Socorro Islands of Mexico. If you are looking for soft, colorful coral, look no further than the islands of Fiji, where God's flower garden awaits; if you are looking for volcanic action, check out the Hawaiian Islands or the hot water from underwater boiling volcanoes off Indonesia; if you like cold water, then maybe you should try the icebergs of Alaska or dive in the Great Lakes.

Each dive location offers something spectacular. All are unique and special to each region of the world. I cannot, for the life of me, say any one location is better than the other; that is why others need to visit as many as they can for a firsthand tour for their own personal experience. My shows simply whet the appetite and make others want to explore the world. The sole purpose of the series is to show others what each location has to offer; then in the end, I let others decide where to go on their next vacation adventure and experience it for themselves.

Most people tend to see pictures of things under the ocean and think it's all the same everywhere, when indeed it is not. Just as Michigan is different from Arizona, and Alaska is different from Florida, every place under the ocean is vastly different as well. When you travel to the different oceans on the planet, you will see that some oceanic mountains are just as large as any you see topside in any part of the world. Some oceans have underwater volcanoes just like you see topside, while others offer some of the most beautiful coral God ever created. My point is that every ocean and sea offer something special for the scuba diver or underwater videographer like me. The scenes are magical.

Speaking of magical, Siegfried and Roy (the renowned German-American magicians and entertainers) spent decades wowing the world with their extravagant illusions involving rare famous white tigers, big cats, elephants, and other animals. Their dazzling visuals put the animal kingdom on stage front and center. I was fortunate to be able to attend one of their "once in a lifetime" spectacular shows while I was in Las Vegas for a Fox Television conference in the mid-1990s. The performers opened their show in a new forty-million-dollar theater built just for them at the Mirage hotel.

I somewhat patterned my work after their magical performances with what I saw deep beneath the oceans once I started filming. After all, it's a kind of "circus" in our oceans with all the performing marine life. The only difference is God's marine life performed free for me, "untrained," and in their own natural habitat. Therefore, I wanted to share with the world these magical incredible performances I witnessed deep below the sea.

God's creations of under-sea mountains, caves, tunnels, cliffs, overhangs, steep walls, and spectacular, colorful reefs and marine life are endless. That is why I know our God is the great Creator. If you think His creations are great topside—and they are indeed—you haven't even begun to witness His creations until you see them below the ocean. Nothing else even comes close. After witnessing the underwater world I have seen firsthand, there is no way scientists or evolutionists can make me believe things just happened to fall into place and evolve as in a big bang theory. Scientists want you to believe this simply because they cannot explain these natural creations and how life developed. They would prefer that we just accept their weak explanations. And when we pin them down, they really have no scientific fact or explanation for how marine animals went extinct or where the original master plan and DNA came from. So, what does all this mean in the end? I have so far shown you the underwater world and how magnificent the oceans, seas, and marine life are on planet earth, which God created. But the ongoing discussion right now goes back to the many scientific theories in trying to determine just how old the world is. Did God create the world in six days as the Bible says in Genesis chapter one? Did God create the heavens and the earth in six days and rest on the seventh day according to Genesis chapter two, verses one and two—a belief held by Christians (referred to as "creationists") around the world? Or was the world created millions and billions of years ago, a theory many scientists tout while going all the way back prior to Darwin, saying that the world was created by evolution over time?

Some highly intelligent, religious scientists say the earth was formed after the great flood covered the whole earth from the Grand Canyon to the depths of the ocean. Very rapid sedimentation formed many layers quickly, which we see in the formation of the Grand Canyon and other parts of the world, where marine fossils are found at the tops of mountains. How did the ocean plant these marine fossils on top of mountains all over the world, if not by a great flood? Creationists show the world was formed in a much shorter time-period—in fact, as little as a few thousand years, maybe six or seven thousand, not by millions of years, as evolutionists proclaim. God told us in Genesis that He was going to wipe out a violent earth with a global flood (Gen. 6:11-17), and the great power of a flood shows what water can do to a planet's surface as we see it today. Think of volcanoes—for example, of what happened at Mount Saint Helens and other areas of the world. Consider what they all do to the planet. Even today, the earth's surface is still constantly changing, and change happens in a matter of days, not millions of years.

Dinosaurs, which are believed to have walked on earth prior to the flood, are found in layers over the earth's surface with bigger bones at the bottom and lighter ones on top. It's as if they just slowly filtered down through the liquid sedimentation found at excavation sites around the world. In fact, scientists have recently even discovered soft tissue in some of the bones. The discoveries themselves are viewed as a method of dating, but they challenge the concept of "deep time," a critical component of evolution. Scientists say soft tissue shouldn't be found in bones that are millions of years old. They would have decayed over that long of a period. Therefore, the Genesis account is the only thing that seems to make sense of it all, that God did indeed create the heavens and the earth in six days (Gen. 1: 1-31). Thus far, through unreliable science, evolutionists have been unable to prove their theory of the world being created over millions of years. I am sure that in due time we will all find out the truth.

For further in-depth evidence, I urge you to see a new and recently released documentary on the subject called *Is Genesis History?* Here are scientists from all over the world, all smart people with PHDs, who study everything from the very makeup of the Grand Canyon to the deepest oceans and the highest mountains, from archeology and unearthed bone discoveries to what the heavens tell us. These brilliant scientists examine in detail every aspect of the universe to prove the Genesis story. There is two competing views but one compelling truth. Philip, a friend over at info@isgenesishistory.com, told me I could insert a plug for the movie here in my book, so here goes. To obtain a copy, go to IsGenesisHistory.com.

I truly hope you enjoyed this book about the creation of the *Dive Travel* series and appreciated and valued my passion and work on the DVD series over the years. This book is a sequel of sorts as a continuation from my first book, *Building the American Dream*, which is still in print at Authorhouse.com. It is also available online at all major bookstores, such as Amazon.com or Barnes & Noble. That book covers my growing-up years on a small dairy farm in the '40s and '50s; it describes what our forefathers went through in those early years, some history of the areas I resided in over the years, the complete history of radio and television broadcasting, the building of a TV station business, and much more.

I thank you for your interest in, and understanding of, God's underwater creations. We all can play a vital role in helping to keep our oceans clean from plastic and other garbage by making sure it stays out of the oceans. We are all challenged to do more than our absolute best to help maintain the ecosystem and the environment despite what man sometimes manages to destroy. Overall, if you take anything away from this book, just remember this. If we lose the oceans, we will lose the world.

If you get a chance to snorkel or go diving, remember to look for God's beauty and His wonders in the deep. God bless, and as always, keep blowing bubbles.

World map of my travels

Chapter 33

Some Final Thoughts and Reflections about Life and Death

Beyond diving, travel, and life itself here on earth, I think each of us needs to reexamine his or her life and begin to think about where he or she is headed, especially as everyone gets older. As we all age, we tend to think we know about everything in life, since it has been passed down from our forefathers from generation to generation. But the truth is, in fact, when we get older, we realize there is far more that we don't know and understand than we have actual knowledge of. Perhaps God's infinite wisdom and mysteries will be explained to us when we make it up to heaven.

I remember as a young person being excited in church, reading the Bible, finding God, and becoming a new Christian early on. I was advised, however, by others that when we get older, we might find ourselves too busy to follow God in our daily lives, and I thought, *Well, that will never happen!* But it did over time when I seemed to least expect it. Suddenly, I got older, got married, and had kids. I know I'm not unusual.

Soon many people with their own lives and expanding, busy careers seem to be preoccupied, and they experience a pause in their relationship with God. While we still go to church, we seem at other times to put God on the back burner, so to speak, and seldom do we have that day-to-day experience with Him we need. I think this decline happens to many of us at some point during our lives, and I am sorry to say it happened to me in my earlier years of adulthood. I am not perfect. I never have been perfect any more than anyone else. After all, the only perfect person who came to earth was Jesus, and He alone is the one we all need to emulate.

I worry today that many aren't committed enough to Him like they should be. Occasionally going to church, volunteering, being nice to people, and donating money to organizations are wonderful. Those gestures of service are all as God intends, but He wants more from each of us, a time of dedication and witnessing to others as Jesus told His disciples to do, to go out and teach all nations. He wants us to witness to others and bring them to Him.

Matthew 10:32-33 says, "Whosoever therefore shall confess me before men, him will I confess also before my Father which is in heaven. But whosoever shall deny me before men, him will I also deny before my Father which is in heaven."

Today we here in America are too preoccupied and busy owning material things, trying to outdo our neighbors, friends, or fellow workers as to how much we can possess. We put way too much emphasis on what we own, on all our earthly possessions, as if they make any of us really any richer in the end. In addition to all our earthy possessions, we buy health insurance, life insurance, car Insurance, fire insurance, even travel insurance. But the one thing that seems to be missing is eternal insurance, and that is one insurance we don't even need to buy with hard-earned cash. It is totally free to one and all, and it is the most treasured insurance of all, yet people fail to understand or accept it.

We can receive it freely by simply accepting Jesus Christ as our Lord and Savior (Acts 16:31; Eph. 2:8), knowing that by putting our faith and trust in Him, we won't just be protected by small insurances here on earth. Instead He promises life eternal in heaven (John 17:3), something far more valuable. That means life forever and ever far from our brief moment of life here on earth, where we live on borrowed time with borrowed items that all belong to God anyway (Ps. 50:10–12; Hag. 2:8; 1 Cor. 10:26).

When Jesus comes again, as He promises in the Bible (John 14:3) during the great resurrection, when all the dead in Christ shall rise first (1 Thess. 4:16), all believers of Christ will live forever and ever in paradise, free from pain and suffering (Rev. 21:4). You will then meet your loved ones, who have gone before you (1 Thess. 4:17), and you will even have a new body in Christ, as promised in 1 Corinthians 15:51–52. But don't procrastinate. Accept Him today (Heb. 4:7). If you should suddenly die in some fatal accident or in a pandemic, it will be too late. You will have missed your opportunity to accept Jesus as your Lord and Savior, and to go to heaven (Jer. 8:20, Matt. 25:10–13).

If you read the Bible, you will see that nearly all the things the Bible has foretold have already come to pass, just as Jesus said (John 14:29). That is why it is called the truth (John 17:17), so why would you doubt the end-time promises Jesus also describes in the Bible? Dear friends, read your Bible. It teaches you and prepares you for life's lessons while you are still here on earth.

John 3:16 says, "For God so loved the world, that he gave his only begotten Son, that whosoever believeth in him should not perish, but have everlasting life."

Romans 10:9 says, "That if thou shalt confess with thy mouth the Lord Jesus, and shalt believe in thine heart that God hath raised Him from the dead, thou shalt be saved."

Many years ago, I used to enjoy watching the Reverend Billy Graham crusades on television and especially hearing George Beverly Shea, my favorite religious singer. Rev. Graham once told of a time, early in his ministry, when he arrived in a small town to preach a sermon. Wanting to mail a letter after arriving there, he asked a young boy where the post office was. When the boy told him, Dr. Graham thanked the boy and said, "If you want to come to the Baptist church this evening, you can hear me telling everyone how to get to heaven."

The boy replied, "I don't think I will be there; you don't even know your way to the post office!"

I have learned from my travels around the world that we are truly blessed here in America compared to those in most foreign countries. The next time you are feeling down in the dumps or feeling sorry for yourself, let the following remind you of just how lucky you really are. Here are some interesting facts in that regard:

- If you have food in your refrigerator, clothes on your back, a roof overhead, and a place to sleep, you are richer than seventy-five percent of this world.
- If you have money in the bank or in your wallet and spare change in a dish, you are among the top eight percent of the world's wealthy.
- If you can read this on your own computer, you are part of the one percent in the world who has that opportunity.
- If you woke up this morning with more health than illness, you are more blessed than the many who won't even survive this day.
- If you never experienced the fear in battle, the loneliness of imprisonment, the agony of torture, or the pangs of starvation, you are ahead of seven hundred million people in the world.
- If you can attend a church without the fear of harassment, arrest, torture, or death, you are envied by, and more blessed than, three billion people in the world.

- If your parents are still alive and still married, you are very rare.
- If you can hold your head up and smile, you aren't the norm; you are unique to all those in doubt and despair.
- If you can read this message, you just received a double blessing in that someone was thinking of you as being very special, and you are more blessed than over two billion people in this world who cannot read at all.

Author Unknown

Count your many blessings, daily received from God.

Jesus came into the world to teach us a four-letter word: love. He died on the cross to prove His love for each of us by dying for our sins (John 3:16). If we could equally spread His love as quickly as hate and negativism, what an amazing world we could live in!

I have met so very many wonderful, caring, and special people around the world over the years in my travels—friends I will never forget. God taught us to love one another, and I could see that love in the faces of so many people I have met from all nationalities, races, and colors, both rich and poor. The world is still full of discrimination. We have come a long way but still have further to go. Discriminating against nonwhite people is a disgrace, a sin; and it's certainly not Christlike. All people are beautiful souls God has made, and I am proud to call them brothers and sisters in Christ.

I have been blessed beyond anything I could possibly comprehend in my life thus far. I have witnessed His vast and mighty, colorful paintings of magnificent corals under the ocean and His undersea mountains, valleys, caves, tunnels, and all the majestic, colorful marine life He created. God has shown me the world and His mighty wonders in the deepest parts of the oceans and seas. How can anyone who goes outside not believe there is a God? The Bible says you can look outside the Bible to believe in God. Look at the sunsets, the mountains, the oceans and be at peace.

Even most evolutionists won't come right out and say there is no God, because the universe is so big; it is millions of light years across. What we occupy here on earth and in our solar system is but a speck of time and matter. The Bible says in Psalm 53:1 that it is a the fool who says there is no God with some certainty. Psalm 19:1 says, "The heavens declare the glory of God; and the firmament shows his handiwork." Romans 1:20 says, "For the invisible things of him from the creation of the world are clearly seen, being understood by the things that are made, even his eternal power and Godhead; so that they are without excuse."

Over the years, God has blessed me by showing me His handiwork throughout the world. Outside of my individual dive shows I just shared with you, I also traveled to many other countries, where I didn't produce a film, but rather I just visited places such as Europe, Singapore, Guam, Japan, Hong Kong, and even China. I even had a chance to visit my nephew, Michael, who is a missionary far away (and his family) in a country I am unable to disclose.

One of my many blessings came in the form of something I never even knew I had been blessed with. Growing up on the farm was a strenuous job as a young boy; farming is a lot of hard work. I had a few minor back pains later in life as I aged from time to time; it was nothing requiring the need for anything as dramatic as surgery, I thought, although I had some doctors and back surgeons tell me over the years that I needed immediate surgery, or I could end up in a wheelchair. That's the kind of information meant to scare one into having such surgery.

The first time was in my late thirties or early forties, when I first noticed something in the form of a little pain in my lower back, but I was told it was spondylitis, an inflammatory, autoimmune condition that typically begins in young adulthood. It is common among a lot of men today. But it never stopped me from carrying heavy objects, which I did over the years from my time as a teenager on the small, rural dairy farm till I ended up making my films around the world for twelve years. I always had way too much heavy luggage to carry with me on those long trips to the other side of the planet. Most of the time I carried three checked bags with me, each weighing seventy pounds; they mostly consisted of dive gear and camera equipment to make my films, plus two carry-on bags in addition, which was a lot to keep track of when I landed and had to retrieve from the baggage claim area. And I was always alone to do just that.

I also carried heavy dive equipment on my back, including heavy tanks, while getting in and out of the water on boats, but somehow I always made it. Of course, I was in better shape back then. In fact, I can remember divers in Australia, guys in their forties, who thought I was much younger than I actually was, at the time in my sixties, because I could lift myself out of the water onto the boat deck with my tank on my back when they appeared to struggle with getting up and out of the water.

Not so long ago, I was eventually referred to a highly recommended back surgeon in a town not far from me. I finally wanted to get some answers to my questions about the back pain I had previously experienced. I made an appointment to see what this was all about. By that time, I was feeling much better, however. What the surgeon told me, though, immediately made me realize that perhaps God had His hand on me in a way no one else could explain. This doctor was one I felt comfortable with from the start and could trust. He was older, and I could feel his smile and sense his Christian presence. That day at his office, I went through the normal X-rays of my lower back, and the surgeon, after reviewing them, came back into the room, placed his hand on my shoulder, and said, "You are a very lucky young man."

I didn't really understand what he meant, but he went on to explain that I had a small bone that had grown up on my lower back, supporting my spinal column. It wasn't normal and was a bone that apparently other surgeons had never noticed. If it hadn't been for that bone growth, he indicated, I surely would have needed back surgery by now, at the very least. His statement sent both excitement and shock through me, not of sorrow but of joy that I had received such a blessing from Someone more powerful than I.

He asked whether I had ever noticed any problems when I was around the tender age of five or seven. Other than the fact that that was about the time I started going to church, I couldn't recall any such problem. Who could remember back to that young age in life? But he said he thought the bone had started about that time in my early childhood. When describing the growth of the bone, the doctor said, "Think of the bone growth as a great glacier, slowly growing all those years of your life to support your spinal column, and it grew at a mere cementer at a time over many decades."

Had that not occurred, I would never have been able to live the normal life of mobility I was blessed with while growing up, including my traveling around the world. He also said he had done hundreds or thousands of operations over the years but could count on only one hand the number of patients like me who had a special bone taking over and growing on its own, correcting my apparent deficiency. He gave me a copy of my X-ray, which showed the bone growth that wasn't part of my original design, a copy which I still have today. So I have proof of its existence. He also warned me before leaving, "Don't ever let anyone do surgery or interfere with what you currently have, or you certainly might end up no longer being able to walk."

I have thought about this issue over the past few years, knowing only God could have blessed and healed me as a small boy, knowing His plan for my life, that I would eventually be traveling and filming His glorious wonders in the deep. Thinking about this, I have come to the conclusion that if He did that for me, healing my bone structure without my knowledge as a young boy, how many of you reading this right now have also been healed and possibly blessed in some similar miraculous fashion and don't even know it? Maybe you were saved during your life from having cancer, a blood clot, a heart attack, a stroke, diabetes, or bone disease? Or perhaps you were prevented from getting injured or killed in a car accident. Maybe He kept you from committing suicide or having some other serious illness unbeknownst to you. How would you even know?

Always thank God for your many blessings, for those known as well as those "unknown." The Bible tells us that God knows all about us from the time before we are born until the time we die (Ps. 139:1–18). Even the hairs on our head are all numbered (Luke 12:7). He alone plans our path forward by opening and closing doors for us. But we must be patient and wait on Him; we cannot question or rush His intent or judgment, but by putting our faith in Christ Jesus, our future lives are in good hands if we accept Him into our lives. God doesn't always immediately answer prayers; after all, He needs to make long-term plans for you; sometimes it takes time. And sometimes He may not answer them at all, but He may instead give you a better plan for your life, one He has creatively designed just for you.

Near the end of my radio career, I lost out on a radio station I had thought and prayed would one day be mine after I had worked hard for it. I grieved over it at the time when It didn't happen. I was told that when God closes one door, He opens another. I wondered what I would do next when the station was sold out from under me, following a sixteen-year career in radio.

Later, I discovered God had a different plan for me, one He had already arranged. He wanted me to have something even greater. It came in the form of a television station He helped us build from the ground up. So never underestimate God's never-ending power (Rev. 19:6) and His guidance in your life (Ps. 32:8; 48:14, Isa. 58:11). Through Him all things are possible (Matt. 19:26; Mark 10:27). Never forget that God isn't bound by present time the way we are (2 Pet. 3:8). We see only the present moment, while God sees everything. We see only part of what He is doing. God sees it all (Job 28:24; 34:21).

Today I continue to show my films to churches, groups, and organizations that invite me to fulfill my promise to God to show all His beauty and creations from where He indeed led me to His wonders in the deep. I have been blessed with three passions in my life to share with mankind. My first passion is my life as a broadcaster in both radio and television. My second is the passion for scuba diving, underwater videography, and film making. And finally, my third, is my passion to spread the message of God's love for the world.

In the end, life simply comes down to this. You have only two masters to choose from in your life (Deut. 11:26–27; 30:19; Josh. 24:15). It is either Jesus or the devil. There is a fight going on for your soul right now. The devil works overtime and extra hard on Christians, trying in earnest to get Christians to become unfaithful and to sidetrack your love for the Lord. The devil doesn't care as much about non-Christians; he already feels he owns their souls unless they immediately change.

Jesus died on the cross to take away the sins of the world (John 1:29); that means "your" sins if you will only repent and ask Him to forgive you (1 John 1:9). The devil, on the other hand, wants to control your life, and he will do anything and everything to keep you from following Jesus. Jesus loves you more than you will ever know (Jer. 31:3). That is why He shed His blood on the cross for you. The devil has done nothing to earn your love; instead he wants to destroy you and fill you with hate and destruction (John 10:10); he wants to destroy anyone who believes in Jesus. He is the same evil one who told Eve to eat the forbidden fruit (Gen. 3:1–6; Rev. 12:9). Satan disguises himself as an angel of light and in many other forms (2 Cor. 11:13–15).

It all comes down to a simple question. Which are you willing to follow? Do you choose good and truth, or do you choose evil and more sin (Deut. 30:15)? Everyone has the choice with the free will God grants. Which will you choose? It is sad to think, after all Jesus did for mankind in shedding His blood on the cross for us here on earth, that so many still refuse to follow Him.

Always follow Christ and put Him first in your life. Believe in Him, and He will always be there for you, just as He has been with me over all these years. Everyone who will accept Him and believe in Him will have life eternally

(John 3:16), and we will someday all meet again after the resurrection in heaven. After all, He is the same Lord and Savior our forefathers got to know through all the years before us (Heb. 13:8). It isn't our competence but rather our character—to be more like Christ—that will get us into heaven.

God bless, and peace be with you!

God's magnificent light streaming down through an underwater cave

Raja Ampat, Indonesia

The following is my *Dive Travel* series DVD list in the chronological order of production:

1. *Beautiful Cozumel, the Drift-Diving Capital of the World* (filmed February 2005, released 2005)
2. *The Caves, Caverns, and Wreck of Cozumel* (filmed February 2005, released 2005)
3. *Key West, a Diving Adventure* (filmed April 2005, released 2005)
4. *Key Largo and the Upper Keys of Florida, a Diving Destination* (filmed April 2005, released 2005)
5. *Bonaire, a Tropical Desert Island* (filmed June 2005, released 2005)
6. *Belize, Home of the Famous Blue Hole* (filmed October 2005, released December 2005)
7. *Fiji* (filmed March 2006, released 2006)
8. *The Great White Sharks of Guadalupe Island, Mexico* (filmed September 2006, released 2006)
9. *Costa Rica on the Pacific Side of the Country* (filmed February 2007, released 2007)
10. *The Turks and Caicos Islands* (filmed February 2007, released 2007)
11. *Southwest Australia, a Diving and Sailing Adventure* (filmed April 2007, released 2007)
12. *Northwest Australia* (filmed April 2007, released 2007)
13. *The Famous Kelp Forest of California* (filmed June 2007, released 2007)
14. *Cocos Island* (filmed July 2007, released 2007)
15. *The Bay Islands of Honduras* (filmed February 2008, released 2008)
16. *Grand Bahama Island* (filmed June 2008, released 2008)
17. *North Carolina Wreck Diving* (filmed June 2008, released 2008)
18. *Shipwrecks of the Upper Great Lakes of Michigan* (filmed August 2008, released 2008)
19. *Manado, North Sulawesi, Indonesia* (filmed November 2008, released 2009)
20. *Nassau, the Bahamas* (filmed January 2009, released 2009)
21. *Revillagigedo Archipelago, Mexico* (filmed February 2009, released 2009)
22. *Anilao, Mabini, and Batangas, Philippines* (filmed March 2009, released 2009)
23. *Curaçao* (filmed April 2009, released 2009)
24. *The US Virgin Islands* (filmed May 2009, released 2009)
25. *Alaska* (filmed June 2009, released 2009)
26. *Raja Ampat, Indonesia* (filmed November 2009, released 2010)
27. *Palau* (filmed December 2009, released 2010)
28. *Aruba* (filmed February 2010, released 2010)
29. *Egypt, Cairo, and the Sinai Peninsula* (filmed June 2010, released 2010)
30. *Egypt, Luxor, and the Eastern Desert Region* (filmed June 2010, released 2010)
31. *Egypt Wrecks of the Northern Red Sea* (filmed June 2010, released 2010)
32. *Truk Lagoon, Chuuk, Micronesia Shipwrecks* (filmed August 2010, released 2011)
33. *Yap, Micronesia* (filmed August 2010, released 2011)
34. *Hawaii: Maui and the Big Island, Part One* (filmed May 2011, released 2011)
35. *Hawaii: Oahu, and Kauai, Part Two* (filmed May 2011, released sept 2011)
36. *Bohol and Palawan Islands, Philippines* (filmed 2012, released 2012)
37. *The Sea of Cortez, Mexico* (filmed 2012, released 2012)

A Sampling of Many Letters of Support and Appreciation We Have Received over the Years

Thank you so much for sending us the copy of your visit to Australia from your "adventure series," which we have enjoyed watching. We hope it serves the US market—a very professional job done very well in great company—you have made a great representation of what you had to work with! The images turned out great and the cutting and sound work. We are very, very pleased with how our business has been represented on the DVD and are delighted to finally see a hard copy. We enjoyed meeting you and will of course welcome your return visit! Have to say, though, I still cringe when I hear myself in my "divers tip of the week"! But, hey, I am not used to being in the spotlight … you did, however, put me at ease! Hope you enjoyed the experience. We shall look forward to seeing you again if you decide to make a revisit anytime soon.
—Erica, Tristan and all the crew at Batavia Coast Dive Academy, Australia

Some months ago, I obtained a copy of your *Key Largo and the Upper Keys Dive Travel* DVD. My sincere compliments for a wonderful video! My parents and I have enjoyed every minute of it. We especially enjoyed your report about the wreck of the *Eagle*. My father was the *Eagle*'s radio officer from 1969–1974. The ship was then known as the *Barok*. My mother and I accompanied him on many travels. I was only a small child at the time, so I don't remember a lot of it. At the end of 2002, twenty-eight years after the *Barok* was sold, and we lost touch; we found out via Google what had become of the ship. Since then I have been skimming the Internet to find as much information, pictures, and other material as possible about the *Eagle*. I have built a website (Eaglewreck.info), on which I try to give as much accurate information about the *Eagle* and its history as possible. Many unique bits of information, photos, and videos are already online there. I would like to ask permission to include your *Eagle* report from the *Upper Keys* DVD on the Eaglewreck.info. Thank you for allowing us in a follow-up letter to display your video. Your love for diving and your desire to show non-divers the underwater world shine through in your productions. Your video will be one of the absolute highlights of my site. I am still a non-diver myself, but I would really like to check out the *Eagle* one day; maybe I could even swim into our old cabin. I found out about your *Eagle* footage when I was searching eBay for "Eagle Wreck." One of the search results was your *Upper Keys* DVD listed on an eBay shop called The Safety Stop. Thanks again, stay in touch, and best wishes.
—Bart Koop-Henzen, The Netherlands

I met Gary in the mid-2000s after a long-time fascination with the TV industry and, in particular, Gary's TV startup, FOX 33 (which you can read about in his other book, *Building the American Dream*). When Gary began producing his *Dive Travel* TV series, I was thrilled to have the opportunity to help with the editing process and the technology behind the scenes. The story of his TV startup was fascinating, and I am sure you will find the next chapter of his life just as interesting.
—Eric Wotila, president, NewsNet, 855-64-NEWS1 x101, Yournewsnet.com

I love the idea of your book. What a wonderful idea! North Carolina's Southern Outer Banks, located near Cape Lookout, offers the perfect combination of the clear and warm waters of the Gulf Stream and the shipwrecks of the Graveyard of the Atlantic. The vast array of shipwrecks from WWI, WWII, and recent artificial reefs provide a variety of habitats for marine life from macro to the Sand Tiger Shark. The German U-boat, *U-352*, sits off our coast and is one of our most popular dive sites. Whether you are into history, marine life, or both, Morehead City, North Carolina, is a must-dive destination.
Best of luck with your book, and let's keep in touch.
—Bobby Purifoy, Morehead City, North Carolina 28557
Robert@olympusdiving.com, info@OlympusDiving.com, OlympusDiving.com

I have had the pleasure of knowing Gary Knapp since 1975 when my wife and I, with our two babies, moved to Cadillac, Michigan, to open a business. The business was a new adventure for us, and Gary stepped up and gave me great suggestions to grow our business. He soon moved on to his own private TV station. With a lot of hard work and very long hours, he built a great TV station that covered northern Michigan. After years of building and owning a successful TV station, Gary sold his business and then found his new passion—diving. With Gary, when he does something, he does it with all his heart. In only a year, he went from being a new diver to a certified dive master. With this behind him, he then decided to apply his photography skills along with his TV background and developed the *Dive Travel* series, which took him all over the world. He was the first to record this underwater series in HD, and his work is second to none; I know, I have enjoyed all the shows. I had always wanted to dive, but due to asthma, I cannot experience it firsthand, but Gary's DVDs have given me the opportunity to see what I would have never seen. I am sure his new book will have you turning pages to learn more about this very talented man and a great friend.
—Bill Cinco, Cadillac, Michigan

Gary, it has been a pleasure meeting you in our worship services at the First Congregational United Church of Christ here in Cadillac. Thank you so very much for honoring us with two marvelous travelogue presentations: *Western Australia* and *Fiji*. These *Dive Travel* journeys were outstanding for our congregation, and here midweek I continue to hear raving reviews of your work. The time frame was perfect (midafternoon), and you were able to get across your material in a fascinating manner, allowing more than enough time for questions from our congregation. I also appreciate the special attention given to "sharks," which are often seen as the most dangerous of all creatures living on the earth. Steven Spielberg put us all on alert with his movie *Jaws*. Now we understand the significance of these aquatic beasts and that without them, the entire ocean ecosystem would be compromised. Since it was a fundraiser for our church and a presentation for our congregation, I am most grateful to you for this wonderful donation. You gave us your time and expertise and along the way helped us raise funds for our church. You are a true blessing to the Cadillac community, Gary, and we are grateful for both the education we have received from these travelogues as well as for your generosity to our First Church congregation. Warmest regards,
—John F. Doud, Cadillac, Michigan

To tell you about Gary Knapp and why you should read this book, I need to share with you my time and experiences with Gary working backward. Today he is a retired CEO of a FOX television station he built from the ground up as well as a retired PADI dive master. He has close to one thousand dives (maybe more) under his belt and has traveled to more places around the world and represents the top 1 percent of people who have done it. Filming the underwater realm to share with everyone he meets is a testament to his passion for diving and for the creatures of the earth.

The Gary I know is a man who tries every day to be a better man than he was the day before. He is a generous man, who is willing to help anyone in need—always willing to give freely of his expertise, his time, or his labor. Gary is a kind man, one of compassion and empathy. More than just highly motivated, I have seen how Gary attacks the day: off to the station, off to film an event in Costa Rica, or off to speak to a small group about sharks, and so forth.

For me to have told you about Gary just as a diver, of which he is an excellent one that I would pattern any new diver after, would be giving you only one side of a multifaceted person such as he. I see him as a man who has, so far, lived two lifetimes and now is discovering a third, retirement—not bad for a guy who once thought some time ago that life was too short and that his looked like it would be that way.

Gary Knapp is driven, not only to experience life but to share his experiences. He is a man I deeply respect, a man who lives by the golden rule. Gary Knapp is a servant of the Lord.
—Morris Langworthy Jr., PADI Course Director, Cadillac, Michigan, Diverscentral.com

These *Dive Travel* DVDs as well as the book *God's Beauty in the Deep* are amazing! Both are enjoyable, relaxing, entertaining, informative, and highly educational. The underwater variety of marine life they reveal, whether plant or animal, is astounding. The clarity is superb. The music is fabulous as well as cultural. The history, geography, and anecdotal stories shared in each of the venues keep your interest and leave you hungry for more. My heart is filled with gratitude for the immense sacrifice in time, energy, and resources it must have taken to provide the world with such a treasure trove of beauty and knowledge that the majority of us would never be able to experience firsthand. Humanity in general, not just divers, should feel indebted to Gary Knapp for creating this series for all people to enjoy and learn from. I cannot wait to share these with my family and friends!
—Rosemary Logsdon Smith, Editor, Sanford, Michigan

My good friend, Gary Knapp, has had the distinct honor and privilege of swimming with some of the most unique creatures of the deep ever created by God. He has sacrificed countless hours over the airwaves and in personal video lectures, sharing their joy and beauty with hundreds of thousands across our great country. His tremendous faith, kindness, and generosity make him special beyond measure. I know you will truly enjoy taking this exciting journey with him into the deep.
Your friend,
—Pastor Trebor Britt, Sarasota, Florida

I have known Gary Knapp for over thirty years. I met him when he owned the TV station and sponsored Christmas craft fairs each year. Since I am a graphic designer, he called upon me to paint the date information on banners that are suspended across our town's main street. Of course, they are mostly all digitally done these days, but back then they were hand-painted with house paint on heavy canvas. Later, I was honored when he called upon me to design the DVD covers for his *Dive Travel* adventures.

The word that best describes Gary is "effervescent." He would come into the shop where I worked and tell me (with much excitement and animation) about his latest adventure. I would then take his many photos and come up with a cover layout that depicted everything he did in that shoot. I could see my coworkers secretly listening as he talked about the many activities and experiences he had while on location. We all envied his exploits!

I don't think Gary is afraid of anything in the water. After he swam with sharks, I asked if he had been scared at all. He simply said, "Oh no. I could swim with sharks any day!" I think the only thing he was a bit hesitant about was when he was asked to shoot a video in Egypt. I could tell he wasn't very excited about the prospect of riding a camel. Of course, for the sake of the video, he did it, but I know it wasn't his fondest experience. Now if camels could swim underwater, I have no doubt, he would be right in there with them!
—Gayle Maurer, Graphic Designer, Cadillac, Michigan

I sincerely recommend both of Gary's books, each for its own reason. His autobiography, *Building the American Dream*, for his inspirational story of his career and business but more importantly the message that a noble purpose and focused hard work are rewarded. His second book, *God's Beauty in the Deep*, is his finest work pursuing a subsequent postretirement diving interest, then sharing it with the world with the context of "what it all means." I encourage you to see the world "topside" and "down under" through *God's Beauty in the Deep* and *Dive Travel* DVDs. I saw the first video episode in one of Gary's presentations. After reading this prerelease manuscript, I can say they are inseparable because of the book's back story. I eagerly look forward to seeing all the dive travelogue episodes. It has been my distinct pleasure to know the author and recommend his works.
—Tom Mejeur, production and marketing, Strong Tower Radio, Cadillac, Michigan

Gary, I am grateful to know you in person. This is a very professional book, and I love this extension of your dive idea. The book explains all the dive scenes, making for a world-class book. All thirty-seven of your DVDs and this book are now mastered together. You are an excellent diver and filmmaker. This is such a great concept, not like any I have seen before. I wish you all the best of luck. Be safe and in good health. Respectfully yours,
—Reto Lingenhag, Zurich, Switzerland

We have seen many of Gary's video adventures in different countries around the world. We found them to be educational and beautiful. Very professionally done with vivid colors of the scenery and God's underwater creations, which most people would never experience. We have appreciated his willingness to share his adventures with us.
—Kern and Chandra Houff, Mt. Crawford, Virginia

We have been living and diving in the Red Sea for approaching thirty years. The apparently barren, desert lands are, in fact, far from that. The phenomenal, historical landscape here holds many secrets of the ancient worlds just waiting to be uncovered. We spent a very pleasurable month with Gary, taking him all over the country to see as much as possible in such a short time. We left the best to the last, though. The magnificent, colorful world under the surface of the Red Sea must be one of our Creator's greatest feats. It is such a testimony to the wealth of the Red Sea that Gary simply couldn't fit it into a single episode and instead created a miniseries of the different regions!

The exciting period came directly after we had the honor to dive with such an intriguing, moral, and passionate journalist, while we had to wait to see if we had managed to do justice to our spectacular country. Gary only films what is in front of him: no setups, no borrowed images. If it wasn't there, you don't see it. We just had to trust that he had captured it all. For sure, we weren't to be disappointed; we were rewarded with an absolutely professional and beautiful record of our times together. Gary is forever in our hearts and is welcome through our doors at any time. Best Regards,
—Steve Rattle, El Quseir, Egypt,+20 1065540888,+44 7958329059
Rootsredsea.com, Pharaohdiveclub.com, Pdctravel.com

Having watched these undersea videos, they fascinated me, yet I dreamed of seeing them with my own eyes. It was very inspiring, so I tried my best to learn how to scuba dive. That gave me a chance to see what was in store in the amazing, real beauty of the sea. It is so wonderful! There is no dull moment, so just enjoy, and watch every segment of the videos!
—Sunny A. Juan, scuba diver, Cavite, Philippines

We love Gary's videos. They take you to a place most of us rarely get to see. They show the beauty of God's creations under the ocean. He is so knowledgeable, and he makes you feel like you are right there. What a great experience!
—Bill and Debbie Dyke, Wooster, Ohio

On behalf of the United Methodist Men, I would like to thank you for your excellent evening presentation to our United Methodist Men and friends' group. Your passion for underwater photography and desire to serve the Lord came in loud and clear. Your announcement of the program generated a lot of interest during the UMC announcements, and Jerry Deer's moving to the larger fellowship hall was a lifesaver that made the event very successful. I think the event was a very successful video presentation of the world, animals, and people God gave us. Praise the Lord. And God bless you. Thanks sincerely.
—Tom Hunt, president of the Cadillac United Methodist Men

Index to the Top Thirty-Seven
Worldwide *Dive Travel* Destinations